HERstory

The Leadership Program

HERstory

A young women's journey of self-discovery through creative writing and dynamic interactive activities

CURRICULUM SUITE

GIRL FRIDAY BOOKS

Copyright © 2022 The Leadership Program

All rights reserved.

Created by The Leadership Program, New York
www.theleadershipprogram.com

The Leadership Program
535 8th Avenue, Floor 16
New York, NY 10018

 GIRL FRIDAY BOOKS

Published by Girl Friday Books™, Seattle
www.girlfridaybooks.com

Produced by Girl Friday Productions

ISBN (print) 978-1-959411-00-0
ISBN (ebook) 978-1-959411-04-8

Printed in the United States of America

Contents

Part Three: Creative Output

Objective: Participants will create an ethnographic theater piece or literary journal that synthesizes their responses and presents the group's writings about identity development as an artistic product.

Epilogue

Objective: Participants will identify and demonstrate appreciation for the HERstory group's accomplishments throughout the year.

Reference

Introduction

Overview

THE LEADERSHIP PROGRAM: WHO WE ARE

For over twenty years, The Leadership Program has worked to provide educational institutions of all types and sizes with youth development activities, professional development workshops, and curricula that help schools expand and enrich their academic communities.

Based in New York City, we serve more than 250 school administrations and organizations nationwide and internationally; we have worked tirelessly to create innovative and engaging curricula that provide schools assistance with youth engagement, parent involvement, management, organization, educational enrichment, strategic planning, and evaluation of their team.

We are highly regarded in the realm of educational consulting and professional development, and are regularly invited to present at national conferences on topics ranging from social-emotional learning to motivating your staff.

The Leadership Program:

- works with over 18,000 students, 500 teachers, and 6,000 parents annually
- created and implements a conflict-resolution project that has been designated the highest-rated leadership-themed universal adolescent violence prevention program in the country by SAMHSA's National Registry of Evidence-based Programs & Practices (NREPP)
- created an empirically validated Conflict Resolution Project, one of thirty-five in the country and designated a Promising Program by the Office of Juvenile Justice and Delinquency Prevention
- was included in a 2008 Johns Hopkins research study for the Department of Defense as one of five organizations in the United States that significantly enhances positive school culture through professional development, organization, and youth development
- created two of the seven programs in New York state (two of the seventy-three in the nation) designated to have Promising Practices by the Academy for Educational Development
- believes that, with the right help, every person has the innate ability to lead the change

HERSTORY CURRICULUM OVERVIEW

HERstory is a yearlong after-school program for adolescent girls composed of Community Building activities and ethnographic theater to promote healthy identity exploration and positive youth development. HERstory emerged out of one practitioner's experience at a middle school in New York City where she "saw the deep need for the predominantly female participants to not just learn to perform but to perform their own stories." The curriculum is based on research on female adolescent development as well as direct classroom experience and application. It has been field tested in urban sites and received accolades from participants, parents, schools, and the after-school field. In 2009, HERstory was one of seven programs in New York state (one of just seventy-three in the United States) designated Promising Practices in Afterschool by the Academy for Educational Development.

This comprehensive curriculum is structured to support both experienced and beginning facilitators in implementing HERstory. Using this manual will help you effectively facilitate the curriculum, ensuring the best possible experience for student participants.

The manual contains twenty-two to twenty-five lessons to be facilitated over thirty-five to thirty-nine sessions, depending on the Creative Output track chosen, and outlines the additional sessions necessary to prepare for the Ethnographic Theater Piece or to create the Literary Journal. All lessons have been designed by The Leadership Program and refined for optimum effectiveness and student engagement. The lessons are organized into three components that engage students in a variety of activities, and are scaffolded to build community and develop trust and cohesiveness within the group, provide avenues for self-reflective writing exercises, and culminate in a full-scale theater production or a literary journal developed from the participants' writings. The components are:

COMPONENT TITLE	OBJECTIVE
Community Building	Participants will create a cohesive, socially and emotionally safe, positive peer group.
Writing Workshop • Identity • Those You Are Closest To • Body Image • Love and Relationships • Dreams • Heritage or Tradition • Legacy	Participants will examine and express their responses to and feelings about multiple aspects of girls' identity development through writing.
Creative Output	Participants will create an ethnographic theater piece or literary journal that synthesizes their responses and presents the group's writings about identity development as an artistic product.
Epilogue	Participants will identify and demonstrate appreciation for the HERstory group's accomplishments throughout the year.

The Writing Workshop component builds through seven themes, from self-awareness to lasting impact on the community and wider world. Each of these seven themes is addressed through three approaches to writing: lesson activities, theme writing prompts, and themed movies with correlated questions to answer. The seven themes are:

- Identity
- Those You Are Closest To
- Body Image
- Love and Relationships
- Dreams
- Heritage or Tradition
- Legacy

All lessons follow the same structure to provide a consistent framework for every session. The lessons open with information and tools to help in your facilitation and continue with step-by-step instructions for each activity.

Each lesson begins with the following information:

- Lesson objective—what students will achieve through the lesson
- Summary—a brief description of the activities during the lesson
- Aim—the question to be answered through lesson activities and processing
- Standards—the Common Core State Standards (CCSS) and Social and Emotional Learning (SEL) standards (based on New York State SEL guidelines) that are met when the lesson is facilitated according to instructions
- Materials—a specific list of the materials to prepare to facilitate each particular lesson, including masters of handouts and worksheets, where applicable
- Handouts—information and reference pages, available for participants in their *Student Writing Companion*s
- Worksheets—activity pages to be filled in by students during lessons, available in the *Student Writing Companion*s
- Vocabulary—significant words used in each lesson, to be incorporated throughout the activities
- Facilitator note—an alert when the lesson requires attention to specific details in preparation for or during the session

The step-by-step instructions are divided into sections within each lesson:

- Prepare in Advance—instruction that appears at the beginning of lessons where effective facilitation requires some materials or activities to be prepared ahead of time
- Warm-Up—a short activity that focuses the group on the session topic and serves as an icebreaker
- Activity—may be divided into two or three parts and includes the activities that go to the heart of the lesson topic
- Closing—a simple format for inviting each student to reflect on how they can use what they have learned during the lesson in their lives

HERSTORY STUDENT WRITING COMPANION

Designed for participating students as a companion to the curriculum, the *Student Writing Companion* provides each student with all the handouts and worksheets they will need for each lesson. The relevant *Student Writing Companion* page numbers are listed in the Materials section at the beginning of each lesson in the teacher manual.

Additional blank pages have been added at the back of the *Student Writing Companion* for participants' drawings, collages, and poems. Participants may want to include some of these writings and art pieces in the group's final script or literary journal, and will therefore want independent access to them before pasting them into the *Student Writing Companion*.

Facilitation Tips

Our facilitation process is built on the experiential learning cycle (ELC), a structured learning sequence that guides multiple styles of learners through experience-based activities (Pfeiffer & Jones, 1975, 1983). Creating continuous threads from one experience to the next, the ELC lets learners process an activity through five stages of comprehension, culminating with concept and skill application. Building on student input and curiosity, facilitators interject well-placed processing questions that allow students to discover each lesson's learning points in a manner that feels organic and seamless. The process has proven successful in all of The Leadership Program's urban school programs and is critical to the effective implementation of HERstory.

Sprinkled throughout each lesson, therefore, you will find:
- Processing Questions—suggested ELC processing questions that apply to the students' experience during the specific lesson
- Discussion Questions—suggested questions to guide the students in reflecting on other aspects of their experience and the topic of the lesson

The suggested questions and prompts are provided to guide students in processing their experience and what they have learned. An effective facilitator will listen attentively to students' comments and responses, and both use these contributions to formulate questions that move the discussion toward answering the Aim or the Closing question and help students apply what they have learned to their lives. You may choose to use the suggested processing and discussion questions that are included, or you may prefer to come up with your own questions based on the group's experience during the session, or you may want to use a combination of the two options. Whichever approach you choose, processing the experience that the students have during the lesson is essential to support participants in expressing themselves on the seven themes in writing and to the success of HERstory.

PREPARATION ESSENTIALS

Space Setup

Some of our activities include games or physical activities, so it is ideal to create an open space in the room.

You may want to have students form a circle to start each lesson. A circle builds community and allows students to easily see and interact with each other.

Setting up particular lights or decor in the style and interests of your participants helps to create a special space for HERstory.

Remember

- Read your lesson ahead of time to decide which arrangement of the furniture will work best for each session. For group interactions, chairs set up in a horseshoe or circle are good. If you will be doing a lot of small-group work, set up chairs in small circular clusters.
- Make sure everyone can see you and any visual aids you may display.

Materials

Always read through the list of materials you will need to facilitate the lesson and prepare your materials in advance to ensure good use of time and smooth running during the session.

If materials include worksheets or handouts, you will find one of each at the end of the lesson from which to make extra copies if necessary.

Suggestion: Complete a sample of each worksheet for yourself before the lesson; you will be able to anticipate any questions that participants may have and make your group feel more comfortable if you provide your worksheet as a sample.

Time Management

These lessons have been created for a two-hour after-school time frame. On days when you have less than two hours, we recommend that you divide the lesson into two sessions. If you read your lessons ahead of time, you will know how to structure the sessions to achieve the lesson objective. Be sure to always leave time to include processing questions to reflect on the lesson experience. If you need help keeping time, set a timer. This will prevent you from running out of time and will ensure that you include the valuable processing portion of the lesson.

Keep in mind that some topics of conversation can get lengthy; monitor the time so that every student who wants to participate has a chance to voice her opinion, and so that the objective for the day is achieved.

Games

The curriculum includes some games, which we believe are the gateway to larger life lessons. Although games to some may not seem like the best use of time, it is important to know that some of your best processing and "aha" moments will come out of these games. They are placed intentionally within the lessons.

Physical Activities

When doing physical activities with your students, always set up a safe space. Make sure that your students are comfortable with the level of physical movement that the activity requires, that there is ample space for it, and that you remind students to keep their own physical limitations in mind when taking part in these activities.

Visualization

Some activities begin with a visualization in which students are asked to close their eyes and imagine a scene that you will describe. It is important, especially the first time you conduct a visualization, to first ensure that all students feel comfortable closing their eyes. If a student does not, he or she can sit quietly with his or her eyes open and gaze turned toward the floor. There should be no talking during visualizations, and students should not touch or otherwise engage each other.

INSIDE THE ACTIVITY

Brainstorm

A brainstorm is used to start conversations or to create a list or a web. It is started by posing a question to the group and then writing down all of the answers given. If you follow the Brainstorming Process Ground Rules, you will prime the group for discussing the day's topic:

- Record all ideas
- No critical judgment is permitted
- Freethinking is welcomed (i.e., the wilder the idea, the better)
- Quantity, not quality, is desired
- Combination and improvement of ideas are sought

Small Group Presentations

Small group presentations occur frequently, when students are divided into pairs or trios to work on something that they will later present to the larger group.

In all group work, let students know how much time they have to work and remind them when to move on to the next person or task. Travel around the room to observe students, to pick up on information for later discussions that students may not think to share with the larger group, and to provide support when needed.

Role Plays

Role plays are used frequently in our lessons. Students act out a specific scene or situation in order to practice skills learned and examine behaviors to choose or avoid. Role plays will provide valuable practice for groups creating a culminating theater piece.

You must set up ground rules for role plays. The most important thing to enforce with your students is that a role play is pretend, and that students are acting a part during the role play. Students should not hash out real-life issues with each other during a role play, nor should they get personally upset with someone's words or actions during a role play. Assign roles thoughtfully to avoid reinforcing negative dynamics between students.

To further reinforce this idea, it is important that role plays have a clear beginning and end. One way to manage this is to have the group call out "3, 2, 1—action!" to begin a role play, and for the facilitator to call out "Scene!" to end the role play. When processing what occurred during a role play, always refer to the students' characters rather than the students themselves. Example: "When Tiffany was playing the customer and said to the store clerk that Cassandra was playing . . ." This helps to further separate the student from the role play.

Web

A web is a visual branching system of words, usually derived from a brainstorm. A web will have a central circle containing a word (the main topic or question) and responses branching out connected by lines, much like a spiderweb. These webs give great visual context to participant ideas. One example is shown below:

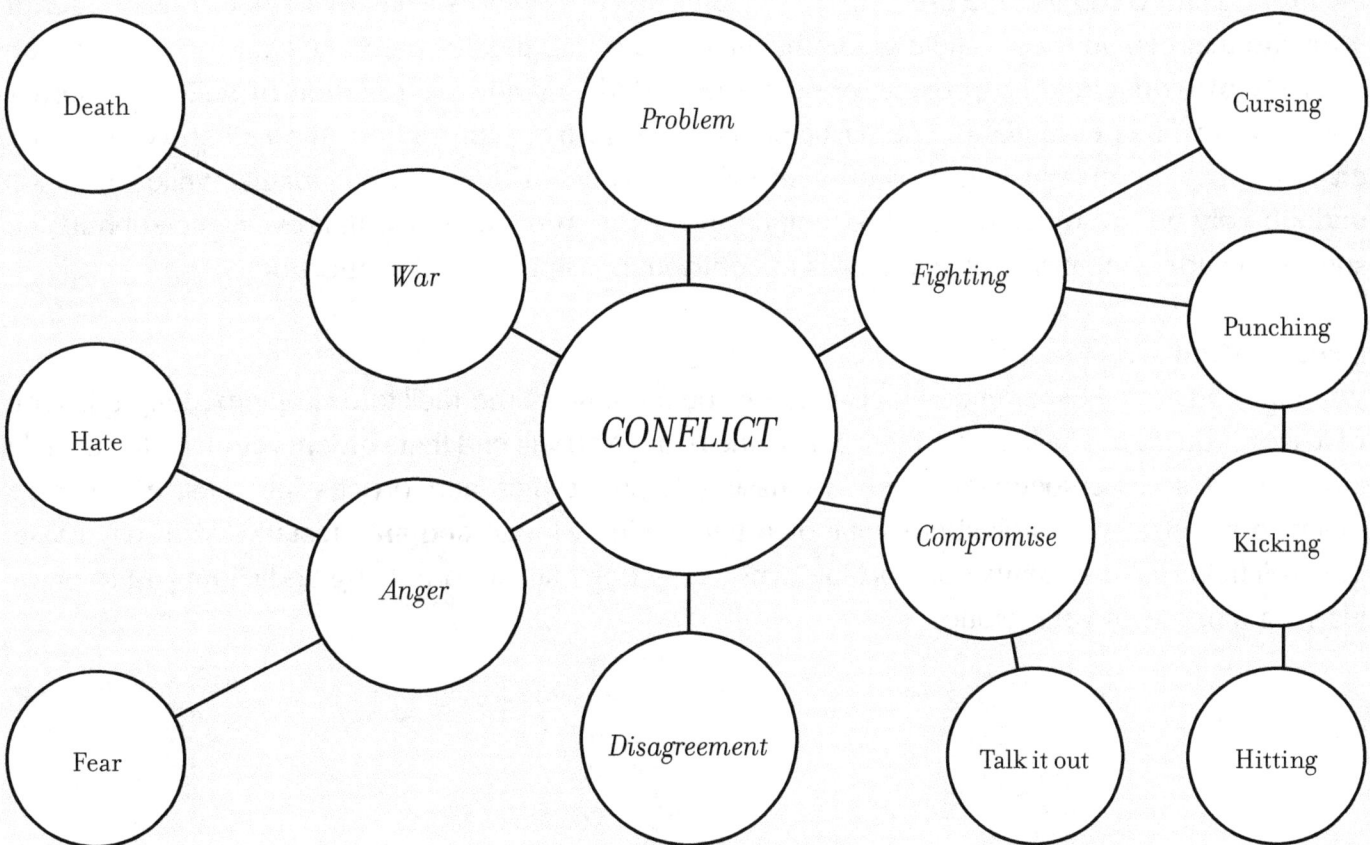

Writing

In addition to the Writing Workshop, writing exercises are incorporated into some of the Community Building lessons so that students can continually practice and hone their literacy skills. These writing exercises also provide an outlet for students who are shy about participating vocally. If students have difficulty with the writing exercises, you can encourage them to write in their native language, draw an image, or find another way to express their response.

The Writing Workshop section provides three approaches to inspiring participants to write: the first approach is through the seven lessons. When facilitated as instructed, the lessons offer poem formats and other options for structured writing. The second approach is the set of theme-based writing prompts that follow the body of each lesson. These prompts pose questions on the theme that participants can answer in a journal style to reflect on the theme. The third approach is to show participants a theme-related movie and have them answer the questions on the correlating movie-response pages. Suggestions for films are included in the Writing Workshop section header. Facilitators can replace these films with their own choice of movies, but should be sure to replace the provided movie-response questions with questions more suited to the chosen film.

Culminating Project

HERstory is designed to culminate with the creation of an Ethnographic Theater Piece and/or a Literary Journal. These artistic products are the expression of the participants' writings and reflections from the various lessons and on the seven themes of HERstory. Four acting lessons are included in the curriculum to support the creation of a theater piece, as well as a link to an electronic file script template that can be used to help guide the structure of the theater piece. Lessons on style and on a variety of writing and art project forms are provided to guide the creation of a literary journal. In both cases, it is essential to use participants' writings from throughout the HERstory program, ensuring that the culminating project is an original piece written by participants. While there will undoubtedly be too much material to include every poem or response that everyone submits, be sure to include each girl's voice and artistic contributions in balanced proportion.

Keep in Mind . . .

Whether you are an experienced facilitator or you are a first-time facilitator implementing this type of lesson, you do not have to be the expert in the room. You will find that students contribute valuable information and perspectives when discussing lesson topics and processing their experience. Maintain a sense of humor about your own gaps in knowledge and any mistakes you may make. This will help make students comfortable when they don't know something and allow you to enjoy learning along with your group.

Part One
Community Building

"The good we secure for ourselves is precarious and uncertain until it is secured for all of us and incorporated into our common life."
—Jane Addams

"I know there is strength in the differences between us. I know there is comfort, where we overlap."
—Ani DiFranco

Community Building

Section Guide

Community Building is essential for fostering a safe environment in which girls can express themselves respectfully and freely, for nurturing genuine bonding among them, and for enabling the group to create a powerful and cohesive Ethnographic Theater Piece or Literary Journal as their final project. The Writing Workshop section that follows will build upon the ideas and themes that emerge throughout the Community Building section, which will in turn lead to the Creative Output section.

The Community Building lessons should be taught in the order in which they appear in the curriculum manual. The syllabus is designed to start with icebreakers and build to trust- and ensemble-building, containing in-depth exploration of both self and community. The curriculum is most effective when the intended design is followed.

YOUR PARTICIPANTS

Style Adaptations: Assess the needs of your group at the beginning of the program to ensure that you select an implementation style for the activities that will yield the most honest and fulfilling results and have the greatest impact for your group. There are suggestions throughout the curriculum that offer adaptations for a more kinesthetic track or a more creative track, depending on the preferences of your participants.

Snack: Whether your group is in middle or high school, a snack remains an important component. Ensure that you are following the school/site protocols for snack administration. Also take into account the needs of your girls such as lunch schedules, program time and duration, snack nutritional value, practical options, school provisions, etcetera. The curriculum asks for intense creative focus; ensuring that your participants have a healthy snack if necessary is important to their energy, mood, and concentration.

YOUR FACILITATION

Opening Ritual: In the first lesson in the Community Building section, there is an important Facilitator Note concerning establishing a consistent Opening Ritual. This Opening Ritual should be facilitated every day before the rest of the lesson begins, preceding any Warm-Up in the curriculum. The goal is to offer the participants a symbolic bridge from their day into the space of the club and the group. The ritual should be centered on self-reflection, and every participant should take a turn. The following are two ritual options. You can adapt either option or devise your own based on the needs of your group.

Opening Ritual Option 1: Rose and Thorn

Rose and Thorn is a whip-around that allows participants to share the high and low points of their day with the rest of the group. Their high point is referred to as their rose and may consist of anything that they are happy about, excited for, inspired by, etcetera. Their thorn, alternatively, is something that bothered them, hurt them, disappointed them, etcetera. For example, "My rose is that my favorite cousin is coming to visit me this afternoon, and my thorn is that my father is out of town and I miss him."

The most important aspect of this ritual is that when it is a participant's turn to share her thoughts, she is the only person who has the floor. It is important to rigorously uphold a "one mic" norm during Rose and Thorn, as it sets the tone for each session, and a peaceful, focused atmosphere is essential for the girls to be able to honestly reflect and share of themselves.

Opening Ritual Option 2: How's the Weather

How's the Weather is a whip-around in which the participant is asked to describe her emotional state using the analogy of the weather. For example, if a participant is feeling overwhelmed, but her friends have been very supportive and have tried to cheer her up, she might say, "My weather today is cloudy with a trace of sunshine now and then." As with Rose and Thorn, the "one mic" norm and a peaceful, focused atmosphere are essential.

Whether it is day one, the day of the performance, or the day of the book party for the Literary Journal, it is important that your Opening Ritual remain the same. This structure allows the participants to have a sense of ownership, and it creates a safe space where the girls know what to expect and where they will each have a moment to be the focus of the group and to share of themselves.

Time Management: Time management is essential to your club session. As it is vital for each of the girls to feel that they are heard, adequate time must be allowed within the activities and during processing for each one to contribute. Keep an eye on the clock and pace yourself throughout the lesson. If time is running short and you feel you have to choose between a closing ritual and continuing an activity a little longer, end the activity earlier and make sure to leave time for the Closing Ritual. It is essential that each girl has a chance to add her voice to the closing every time the club meets. Each lesson bridges to the next and cannot adequately transition without processing the experience the girls had that day or without a consistent closing.

Processing: Remember that the key to a successful lesson is not the perfect completion of an activity. The heart of a lesson lies in processing what took place on this particular day with this group of participants during the activity. There are numerous suggested processing and discussion questions within the curriculum to facilitate, and the experiential learning cycle, which is described in the Reference section at the back of the book. It is vital to follow the structure of the experiential learning cycle to facilitate students' comprehension and engagement in the experience. You may adapt the specific questions based on the group's needs and the flow of the discussion. If an unplanned opportunity to offer insight to participants arises during the lesson, you may want to take advantage of this teachable moment to begin processing, because it may yield important revelations. You can return to the written processing structure for closure at the end of the activity.

YOUR SPACE

Creative Environment: Equally important as the verbal rituals in your group are the rituals that occur nonverbally within your space. Setting a warm, inviting, creative, and inspiring ambiance is essential to the establishment of a feeling of community and security. For example, do you always have the lights set a certain way when the students enter? Do you always have music playing for the first ten minutes as they arrive? How do you create the environment you want the girls to experience when they arrive for the club?

Decorating the Space: It is important to assess the character and culture of your group and, where possible, adapt the room's decor accordingly. Depending on the vibe, energy, and style of your group, this can be in the form of student artwork, posters, string lights, plants, inspirational quotes or photos, etcetera. Thoughtfully chosen measures that have a transformative effect on the space have proven to be highly effective in promoting student engagement.

Taking Ownership of the Space: Creating a sense of ownership over the space for the participants is essential even if the room is used for alternate purposes (e.g., as a classroom) during the day. While the group inhabits the space, it should feel dedicated only to HERstory. To accomplish this consistently, consider the following questions: Are you able to enter the room before the girls arrive? Do you have keys, if necessary? Are you able to keep the Tree of Growth referred to in the Welcome to HERstory! lesson showcased in the room? Are the Circle of Hands norms created in the same lesson and the **HERstory Code** poster from the R.E.S.P.E.C.T. lesson displayed visibly so they may be referred to often? Are you able to arrange the room at the start of each club session (e.g., set chairs in a circle)?

Responsibility for the Space: Sharing the care of the space in a respectful way is very important to the culture of HERstory. Depending on the needs and options at your site, you may want to assign certain rotating tasks to the participants so that the girls are equally responsible for the space's care. The tasks can be arranging the chairs, packing up the art supplies, picking up litter, sweeping the floor, etcetera. If the space is used by others, then part of your closing should be devoted to returning it to its previous configuration. This also may provide a kinesthetic opportunity for daily closure for your participants. If the space is solely devoted to HERstory, a ritual should still be devoted to returning it to a certain configuration to prepare for the next session.

YOUR PREPARATION

Preparation and Materials: Always read the lesson thoroughly ahead of time, a day or more before you plan to facilitate it, so you have time to gather materials, prepare samples if called for, and ensure that you have sufficient materials/copies for your number of participants. As noted in the curriculum, it is important to have flip chart paper, markers, and masking tape for each lesson.

Facilitator Notes: Read all Facilitator Notes within the lesson carefully. These are based on experience implementing this curriculum, and they are provided to help you have a successful lesson.

Prepare in Advance: Some lessons include a Prepare in Advance note under the Materials list. These notes call for you to prepare a special activity or a writing or creative sample for an activity. Be sure to have your activity or sample prepared before you begin the lesson so that the girls understand clearly what is being asked of them. Modeling the activity is essential for student engagement and promotes their creativity and ownership of the assignment, as well as their willingness to take risks outside their comfort zone.

Facilitator Worksheet Samples: Review worksheets that are included in lessons so that you will be prepared to answer participants' questions about them. We suggest that you fill out a sample worksheet before you facilitate the lesson to familiarize yourself so your focus can remain on the girls while they are experiencing the activities.

Student Writing Companion: The *HERstory Student Writing Companion* is a complementary volume to the HERstory curriculum manual. The *Student Writing Companion* contains all the worksheets and handouts from every Community Building section lesson, as well as all the Writing Prompts and Movie Response Questions from the Writing Workshop section, and pages for drawings and reflections from the Creative Output section. We strongly recommend a *Student Writing Companion* for everyone in your group, so that each girl has a central location where she can keep her work and a tangible record to take with her at the end of the program. This curriculum manual contains the worksheets and handouts as well, so that if a girl needs additional or replacement pages, you have a source from which to copy them.

Welcome to HERstory!

OBJECTIVE
Participants will define their HERstory community and determine a ritual for connectedness.

SUMMARY
Through hands-on activities, participants determine the environment they want to create for their HERstory community.

AIM
How can we build a HERstory community?

STANDARDS
CCSS – RI.7, W.3, W.4, SL.1, SL.2, SL.4, L.6
SEL – Self-Awareness, Self-Management, Social Awareness

MATERIALS
flip chart paper, markers, masking tape, supplies for the HERstory Pledge Ritual activity of your choice (e.g., two different-colored roses per participant, or a potted plant and jelly beans).

Lesson Vocabulary

brainstorming n., a conference technique of solving specific problems, stimulating creative thinking, and thinking of new ideas

community n., a group sharing common characteristics or interests, perceiving itself distinct from a larger group

connected adj., united, joined, or linked

expectation n., the act or state of looking forward to or anticipating

pledge n., a solemn promise or agreement to do or refrain from doing something

ritual n., an established or prescribed procedure that is practiced

PREPARE IN ADVANCE
Using the Community Building Section Guide at the beginning of part one, choose ahead of time the Opening Ritual you will facilitate at the beginning of every HERstory session for the duration of the residency. Two suggestions are included, or you may create your own ritual that gives each girl a voice at the start of every lesson.

 ## WARM-UP :: INTRODUCTIONS AND ICEBREAKERS

Part 1: Name Introduction
• Ask girls to state their names and one reason why they want to be a part of this HERstory group.

Part 2: Program Description
• Explain how the HERstory program is going to be implemented at your site. Include background information on HERstory, as well as schedule, expectations of this HERstory community, final creative product, eligibility, and commitment, where appropriate.

Part 3: Ritual Icebreaker
• Facilitate the Opening Ritual you have selected and prepared in advance.

 **ACTIVITY ONE :: CIRCLE OF HANDS**

Part 1: Brainstorm
- Review the Lesson Vocabulary with participants.
- Explain: "It's important for us to establish a set of norms to uphold in our classroom or group community."
- Ask participants if they can think of other communities that may follow norms.
- Record their ideas on the flip chart paper.
- Tell the participants that each class/session will involve open discussion and sharing.
- Explain that one of our goals as a community is to make sure everyone's voice is heard.
- Tell the participants that today we are going to establish and agree on a set of classroom norms.
- Place a new piece of flip chart paper on the wall or on a table.
- Ask participants to come up and trace their hands in a circle on the paper, leaving space both inside and outside of the circle of hands for writing.
- Tell participants that the circle represents the community of the group.
- Ask the group to brainstorm negative behaviors we often demonstrate when we are communicating with each other (e.g., talking out of turn, laughing, judging or making fun of someone based on their opinions or beliefs).
- Record the ideas on the flip chart paper in the space outside the circle of hands.
- Ask participants to brainstorm positive behaviors we should demonstrate when we are communicating with each other (e.g., taking turns, being respectful to one another, fully listening to each other).
- Record ideas on the flip chart paper in the space inside the circle.

Part 2: Agreement
- Inform the group that behaviors listed inside the circle of hands represent our community norms and will be modeled in class.
- Tell them that behaviors listed outside the circle of hands represent negative behaviors that will be left outside this classroom.
- Allow the group a few minutes to review the entire brainstorm list.
- Ask the participants if there is anything they would like to remove from or add to the brainstorm list.
- Ask everyone to come up and sign their name on one of the hands composing the circle as a symbol of their agreement to uphold the norms they have just brainstormed. Let them know they can choose any hand to sign their name in and that there can be more than one signature within any hand.
- Once the entire class has signed, have participants return to their seats.
- Tell the participants that they will be responsible for holding themselves and the rest of the group accountable to these norms and that you will review the classroom norms as needed during each session.
- Have participants briefly share ideas for respectfully holding one another accountable to the norms. For example, if participants are talking out of turn, you could remind them that doing so is something that should be left outside the classroom.
- Record participants' ideas for respectfully holding one another accountable on the board or flip chart paper, and post the chart prominently in the classroom.

 **PROCESSING QUESTIONS**

1. *How did it feel to brainstorm how we want to treat one another?*
2. *Was it difficult or easy to come up with positive and negative behaviors? Why?*
3. *Why is it important to have clearly defined norms/guidelines?*
4. *Why is it important to hold one another accountable to norms?*
5. *Where else in your life do you apply a set of norms?*
6. *How do norms encourage positive or effective communication?*

 **ACTIVITY TWO :: SWITCHING PLACES**

- Have participants sit in chairs in a circle.
- Important: There should be the exact number of chairs for the number of participants in the room, excluding you. No chair should be available for you.
- Remind participants that in this activity, as in all the HERstory activities, anything said is confidential.
- Stand in the center of the circle.
- Explain that in this game there will be no pushing or shoving. If anyone gets hurt, the game will end immediately.
- Tell the group that the person in the center of the circle has to say one true thing about herself that is visible (i.e., true about her physical person), but must state it in the following example format: "Anyone wearing blue, switch places."
- Instruct the seated participants that if the statement is also true for them, they must get up from their seat and find another. They may not stand up and sit down again in the same seat on the same turn.
- Instruct participants to say their "switch places" statements loud enough and slowly enough for everyone to hear, so that others will know whether the statement is true for them.
- The person left without a seat in each round should stand in the center and say her "switch places" statement—something true about herself that is visible—using the wording in the example format.
- After several rounds of the game, raise the stakes by instructing a student in the center to say one true thing about herself that cannot be seen (e.g., "Anyone who was born in New York, switch places").
- After several more rounds, raise the stakes again by telling the participants that now when they find themselves in the center, they should give an opinion or share how they feel about something (e.g., "If you think Kanye is the best hip-hop artist, switch places").
- Finally, increase the risk-taking to the highest level for this activity by instructing the participant in the center to tell the group something that is true about herself the group might not know (e.g., "Anyone who ever hurt a friend's feelings, switch places") or share an opinion or feeling (e.g.: "Anyone who ever felt scared, switch places").

FACILITATOR NOTE

You may find it easier to create a smooth transition between risk levels in this game when you play the game also. You can place yourself in the center after a few rounds at each level, so that you can announce each transition and model an appropriate statement for it. As you move through the levels, encourage participants to make statements that have significance and share something about themselves that really matters to them, but not to violate their boundaries.

PROCESSING QUESTIONS

1. *What was playing this game like for you?*
2. *Who enjoyed being in the center of the circle? Why?*
3. *Who did not enjoy being in the center of the circle? Why?*
4. *How did people get seats? What did you notice about how the group as a whole acted physically?*
5. *What did you discover about yourself?*
6. *Did anything surprise you? What? Why?*
7. *What did you find you had in common with others in the group?*
8. *Ask yourself without answering aloud: Were you honest about yourself?*
9. *How did this activity affect you as a member of this group?*
10. *How can this experience help you in this or other groups?*

ACTIVITY THREE :: HERSTORY PLEDGE RITUAL

Part 1: Creating the Ritual

FACILITATOR NOTE

Depending on the needs of your group, this HERstory Pledge Ritual can take many forms. The objective is to create a symbolic and kinesthetic activity that serves as a group pledge of intent for what the girls would like to get from and give to the program. Included below are two suggestions:

- Rose Activity: Participants are given two roses, each a different color. With music playing at a low volume, the girls should stand in a circle (the circle can be surrounded by a string of lights laid around on the floor or other visual symbols to set off the ritual space in a special way, if desired). In round one, each participant places one colored rose in the center of the circle and states one thing that she would like to learn in HERstory this year. Then, in the second round, each participant places the second colored rose in the center and states one thing she would like to give to the HERstory group this year. Keep the rose pile in place or set off to the side until the end of the session.

- Tree of Growth: Participants stand in a circle. A potted tree (or a plant that represents a tree) is placed in the center of the circle. Participants are each given two jellybeans or equivalent seedlike items. In the first round, going around the circle, each girl has the opportunity to state one thing that she would like to learn in HERstory this year. She then plants one of her jellybeans/seeds. In the second round, each girl plants the second jelly bean and states one thing she would like to give to the HERstory group this year to help it grow. The tree is kept in the HERstory space and tended to by the group as the year progresses.

Part 2: Letter to Yourself

- Explain to the girls that they will now infuse everything they have learned from the introduction and ritual into a letter that they will write to themselves.
- Tell them that each girl will compose a letter addressed to herself and in it will include her hopes and dreams for her experience in HERstory this year.
- Let the participants know that, if they so desire, one of the seed-metaphor items or a few petals from their roses can be included in the envelopes.

- When she finishes writing, have each girl seal her envelope and sign her name across the envelope's flap. **Note:** Individual flair can be incorporated into the final stage of completing the letters (e.g., glitter can be sprinkled into the envelopes, or envelopes can be secured with a wax seal).

 **CLOSING :: WHIP-AROUND**

- What is one thing you hope to learn in our next HERstory meeting?

Guess Who I Am

OBJECTIVE
Participants will identify positive attributes about themselves and each other.

SUMMARY
Participants will share with the class positive information about themselves in the form of a game.

AIM
What are some positive qualities that we have in common?

STANDARDS
CCSS – RI.7, W.4, SL.1, SL.2, SL.4, L.6
SEL – Self-Awareness, Social Awareness

MATERIALS
index cards, blank pieces of 8½ x 11 paper, markers, stickers, A "Me" Inventory worksheet (p. 2 in the Student Writing Companion)

Lesson Vocabulary

attribute n., a quality or characteristic that describes someone or something

WARM-UP :: THE STORY OF YOUR NAME

- State the Aim of today's activity.
- Review the Lesson Vocabulary with the group.
- Have participants sit in a circle.
- Ask participants to think for a moment about a story involving their name, based on a topic such as:
  - How they got their birth name or a nickname
  - A name that people always confuse with their name
  - Someone they were named after
- Instruct each participant to state her full name and the story behind her name. If a participant cannot think of a story, she should use her imagination to make up a story.

ACTIVITY ONE :: GUESS WHO I AM

Part 1: Making Index Cards
- Hand out an index card to each participant.
- Tell participants not to write their name on the card.

- On the index card, ask participants to finish these five statements about themselves:
  1. One thing I am good at is . . .
  2. One thing I would like to learn is . . .
  3. One dream I have is . . .
  4. One thing I am scared of is . . .
  5. I stand up for what I believe in because . . .
- Remind participants to write neatly so that others can read their answers.

Part 2: Guessing Game
- Collect the index cards.
- Shuffle the cards and randomly pick a card to read aloud to the class.
- Explain that participants should raise their hand if they can guess who wrote the card. Give the class three guesses before you ask the author to raise her hand by saying: "Will the mystery person please raise your hand?"
- Have that participant pick the next card and read it aloud to the class. The class again has three guesses.
- Repeat the process until everyone's card has been read.

OR

- Collect the last three cards and have the three uncalled participants come to the center of the circle.
- Randomly give each of them one of the cards.
- Have each participant read aloud the cards she was given.
- After all three cards have been read, choose a volunteer from the class to come up and match each card to its correct author.
- Repeat this matching with new volunteers until each of the last three participants is paired with her card.

 **PROCESSING QUESTIONS**

1. *What happened when you filled out your card?*
2. *How did it feel to come up with these five statements about yourself?*
3. *What happened in the group?*
4. *Were you able to identify your fellow participants by their cards? Why or why not?*
5. *Did you learn anything new? Did anything surprise you?*
6. *Now that we've listened to everyone's statements, do you feel any differences in our group from when we started today?*

Part 3: A "Me" Inventory
- Refer students to **A "Me" Inventory** worksheet.
- Have participants complete the worksheets.
- Tell participants to pair up to share their responses.
- Ask each pair to share with the class one thing they discovered that:
  - They have in common
  - Is different
  - They can support each other with (e.g., one is a good cook and can teach the other some

simple recipes; the other is good in math and can help her partner in that subject)

ACTIVITY TWO :: INTERVIEWS

- Divide the group into pairs.
- Tell participants they are going to interview each other.
- Give participants guiding questions to ask their partners. Three sample questions are:
- What is one character trait you wish you had more of?
- What is one thing that you are proud of?
- Who is the person who has had the strongest influence on shaping your character?
- Ask participants to present their interviews to the group.

PROCESSING QUESTIONS

1. *How did it feel to interview your partner?*
2. *How did it feel to answer questions about yourself?*
3. *Why did we ask you to recount your partner's answers instead of having her tell us herself?*
4. *Where else are we called upon to gain information about other people?*
5. *What does learning about someone else bring to the group?*

CLOSING :: WHIP-AROUND

- What is one thing your partner said during the interviews that you will remember?

A "Me" Inventory

THREE THINGS I DO EXTREMELY WELL: 1. 2. 3.	THREE THINGS I DO OKAY: 1. 2. 3.	THREE THINGS I DO, BUT WOULD BE EXTREMELY HAPPY NEVER TO DO AGAIN: 1. 2. 3.
THREE THINGS ABOUT MYSELF THAT I REALLY LIKE: 1. 2. 3.	THREE THINGS ABOUT MYSELF THAT ARE OKAY: 1. 2. 3.	THREE THINGS ABOUT MYSELF THAT I WISH I COULD CHANGE: 1. 2. 3.
THREE GOOD THINGS OTHER PEOPLE THINK ABOUT ME: 1. 2. 3.	THREE THINGS THAT OTHER PEOPLE THINK ABOUT ME THAT ARE OKAY: 1. 2. 3.	THREE THINGS THAT I WISH OTHER PEOPLE DIDN'T THINK ABOUT ME: 1. 2. 3.

 Bonus: After filling out the grid, put a star next to all the items that you can control (e.g., I'm a good friend). Put a zero next to all the items you can't control (e.g., I like the color of my eyes).

R.E.S.P.E.C.T.

OBJECTIVE

Participants will define the concepts of self-respect and respect for a community.

SUMMARY

Participants define the concepts of self-respect and respect through an artistic activity and a game.

AIM

How do you respect yourself and a community you are part of?

STANDARDS

CCSS – RI.7, W.4, SL.1, SL.2, SL.4, L.6
SEL – Self-Awareness, Self-Management, Relationship Skills

MATERIALS

*your own Name Drawing example, at least eight balls (or other tossable items) to use in Cooperation Toss, a whistle (optional), flip chart paper, two markers, a stopwatch or watch with a second hand, the **Respect Yourself!** worksheet (p. 3 in the Student Writing Companion), **HERstory Code** poster (print from the following URL: http://theleadershipprogram.com/ script-template-code)*

Lesson Vocabulary

code n., any system or collection of rules and regulations

respect 1. n., a feeling or attitude of admiration and deference toward somebody or something; 2. v., to pay due attention to and refrain from violating something; to show consideration and thoughtfulness in relation to somebody or something

self-respect n., belief in your own worth and dignity

PREPARE IN ADVANCE

Complete your own Name Drawing to use as an instructional model for the girls.

We recommend that you prepare a poster-sized board or chart paper on which to write the HERstory Code, which should be displayed throughout the program. The Leadership Program's poster design suggestion is included at the end of the lesson. If you have a poster printer, you can print a poster size of this design by going to the following URL: http://theleadershipprogram.com/script-template-code, and printing it from the poster printer. Alternately, you can create your own design or have the girls in your group design a poster. Be sure the design includes enough space for the HERstory Code norms and for the girls' signatures.

 ## WARM-UP ONE :: NAME DRAWINGS

* Pass out a blank piece of paper to each participant.
* Explain to the group that they will be making name drawings.
* Explain that the key to the exercise is in how they draw their name. Tell the students that how

they write their name and decorate the paper should be symbolic of their character and personality.

- Show the class your prepared name drawing.
- Ask the following questions to get participants started, or ask them when they present their finished drawings:
  - What colors will/did you use?
  - Will/did you write your name small or big, bold or light?
  - What objects or symbols will/did you include?

 ## WARM-UP TWO :: COOPERATION TOSS

- Have participants stand in a circle.
- Explain the goal of Cooperation Toss: to have as many balls as possible thrown and caught at one time. In theory, there is nothing limiting the number of balls that can be thrown and caught besides the number of people in the group.
- Spell out the following rules:
  - Everyone must hold her position in the circle.
  - The group starts with one ball to toss.
  - There is no talking except to give the signal to throw the ball, which is: "One, two, three." The group says this together each time. Any other talking results in the group losing a ball.
  - Whoever is holding a ball on "three" must throw it to someone else in the circle, and that person must catch the ball.
  - Anyone in the group may start the "One, two, three" signal, but once it starts, everyone must join in and throw on "three." Otherwise the round does not count.
  - Three consecutive successful rounds means the group gets to move to another level and gets another ball. Three unsuccessful rounds and the group loses a ball. If two balls hit in the air, both balls are lost.
  - The group is allowed three short strategy sessions in which participants can talk about the game. If someone thinks the group needs a strategy session, she raises her hand and the play stops. If others agree to this, they also raise their hands. If they disagree they keep their hand down. The whole group must agree to the strategy session; if one person doesn't raise her hand, there is no strategy session and play must resume.
  - Other important rules of the game: No speaking, no touching, and no hitting someone with a ball.
  - Allow the group as many tries as time allows. Remind them that this game can be repeated in later classes to allow them a chance to better their success.

 ## DISCUSSION QUESTIONS

1. *Was this game easy or challenging? Why?*
2. *What strategies did you employ in this game? Were they successful? Why or why not?*
3. *Did the experience of the game remind you of any other situations in your life?*
4. *Would the same strategies you used in the game work in these situations?*

ACTIVITY ONE :: RESPECT YOURSELF

Segue: Explain to participants that: "Working together to face challenges in a respectful way is essential to our growth as a HERstory community. Therefore, in our second activity today, we will focus on what it means to respect both ourselves and each other."

Part 1: Self-Respect Is . . .

- Ask the participants what they think respect is and let them call out several answers.
- Ask: "Who is the most important person for you to have respect for in your life?" Solicit answers until someone says "Yourself."
- Explain that the next game the group will play is going to address the question of how a person respects herself.
- Review Lesson Vocabulary.
- Divide the class into two teams.
- Give each group one piece of blank flip chart paper, and have them designate a team member who will write down the ideas.
- Tell each team to take one minute to brainstorm ways they can respect themselves.
- Next, explain to participants that during the game, only one representative for each team will play against one representative from the other team, with the option of being substituted by one backup.
- Before playing, tell each team to decide who their representative will be and who their backup will be.
- Explain that the two players (one for each team) will alternate completing the phrase "Self-respect is . . ." with a concrete thing someone would do to respect herself. These things should come from the list brainstormed with the team or off the top of the representative's head.
- Have each team elect a scribe who will keep track of their players' answers as the game is being played.
- Tell participants that the piece of flip chart paper with brainstormed ideas will not be accessible to the representative during play, although it may be accessible to the team for use in the lifelines (see below).
- Also tell the participants that no ideas may be repeated, even if both teams had the same idea on their lists. Emphasize that the rest of the team may not yell out ideas while the player is playing.
- Explain that when one player hesitates for more than five seconds in completing the phrase, you will blow the whistle.
- Let them know that once the whistle is blown, the player who hesitated has three lifelines to choose from:
  1. She can ask one member from her team for one idea.
  2. She can request a group huddle for fifteen seconds to solicit more ideas from her team.
  3. She can tag out and be replaced by her backup for the remainder of the game.
- Explain that each team can get only three strikes (hesitations). The first team to get three strikes becomes the runner-up, and the other team wins. Emphasize, however, that the point of the game is brainstorming answers to the question "How do you respect yourself?" Therefore, it is of little importance which team finally "wins."
- Repeat the game for the phrase "Respecting each other means . . ."

FACILITATOR NOTE

The game should move very quickly; keep the energy up and the ideas flowing. Plenty of time should be left at the end for discussion of the ideas that come up during the game. Also, the amount of time given to a participant who hesitates before the whistle is blown can be varied according to the needs of the class.

 **DISCUSSION QUESTIONS**

1. What was it like to come up with ideas in your group?
2. What was it like to come up with ideas while playing the game? What was it like to represent your team? What was it like to watch your team's representative play?
3. How did your experience of the game affect your self-respect? What about your respect for each other?
4. Which of the ideas that were mentioned in the game do you think were the most important for showing yourself respect?
5. Were there any important ways to respect yourself that we left out?
6. Is there a difference between having self-respect and being self-centered or thinking you're "all that"?
7. Is it necessary to have self-respect before you can respect others?
8. What are ways we can show each other respect?

Part 2: Respect Yourself!
- Have participants complete the **Respect Yourself!** worksheet.

 **PROCESSING QUESTIONS**

1. What happens when people don't respect themselves?
2. Why is it important to treat yourself with respect?
3. What is an example of a time you didn't treat another person with respect?
4. What is an example of a time you showed someone else respect?
5. Are there situations where other people in your life pressure or encourage you not to treat yourself with respect? Why do they do so? How do you usually respond?

 **ACTIVITY TWO :: HERSTORY CODE**

- Display the Circle of Hands flip chart paper you created together during the first lesson.
- Tell the girls that together you are going to create a set of group norms to live by for the duration of the program to ensure that the respect you have just discussed becomes a part of your HERstory culture.
- Ask the girls to take into consideration the discussions about community culture that have taken place over these first three days of HERstory as well as the Circle of Hands activity.
- Brainstorm a set of norms/a code with the group. Discuss what the word "code" means and what it means to live by a code. Review the vocabulary definition.
- Review the brainstorm and see what can be pared down (e.g., words that mean the same thing or can be expressed by one word chosen by the group).

- Tell participants they will be held accountable for this code both inside and outside the club.
- Once the code is finalized, transcribe it onto the provided HERstory Code poster.
- Have all participants sign the poster and hang the poster in the classroom.

FACILITATOR NOTE

These norms should be designed to promote the community solidarity and the socio-emotional health of the group. Avoid any negative terminology. Norms should not be centered on what can't happen but instead what should happen. Here is an example of a HERstory Code from a school in Washington Heights, New York:

1. *We are family—be kind to and respect each other.*
2. *Accept people for who they are.*
3. *Everyone's voice counts.*
4. *Be courageous—show your true colors. Be true, be you.*
5. *Be tolerant of each other—we are here to tell our stories.*
6. *Be generous with your time, your words, and your heart.*
7. *Fly free—let your imagination soar.*
8. *Faith, trust, and pixie dust!*

 **CLOSING :: WHIP-AROUND**

- Which line of the code were you most affected by today and why?

Respect Yourself!

1. Choose one of the ways to respect yourself that came up in the game today that you do *not* already do and that you can commit to doing between now and the next HERstory session. Write it below.

   One way I will respect myself is by _____
   _____

2. What do you think it will be like to respect yourself in this way?
   _____

3. Do you think you can commit to respecting yourself in this way on a regular basis? Why or why not?
   _____

4. What are three things you already do in your life to respect yourself?
   1. _____
   2. _____
   3. _____

5. What are three things you don't do but would like to do to respect yourself?
   1. _____
   2. _____
   3. _____

6. What do you feel is the main thing that gets in the way of you respecting yourself?
   _____

HERstory Code

Human Spectrum

OBJECTIVE
Participants will identify and practice communication skills.

SUMMARY
Participants use communication skills in a group activity.

AIM
How can we work together successfully as a group?

STANDARDS
CCSS – RI.7, W.1, W.4, W.7, SL.1 – SL.4, L.6
SEL – Self-Awareness, Self-Management, Social Awareness, Relationship Skills

MATERIALS
*masking tape, flip chart paper, markers, **Sample HERstory Spectrogram Questions** and **HERstory Human Barometer Statements**, Diversity Pursuit worksheet (p. 4 in the Student Writing Companion)*

Lesson Vocabulary

barometer n., an instrument for determining the pressure of the atmosphere

opinion n., a belief or judgment held with confidence but not substantiated by proof

persuade v., to cause somebody to adopt a certain position, belief, or course of action

point of view n., a mental perspective or outlook; your personal way of looking at the world

spectrogram n., a graphic representation of a spectrum

spectrum n., a continuous sequence or range

FACILITATOR NOTE
For both the Spectrogram and the Human Barometer activities, use masking tape as a visual aid. To begin the exercise, stretch a piece of masking tape across the middle of the room. This may help the participants visualize where they are on the line for each question.

PREPARE IN ADVANCE
Create an acronym for "friends" on a piece of flip chart paper. For example:
F Fun
R Reliable
I Interested in listening
E Effort
N Needs communication
D Dependable
S Safety

WARM-UP :: ONE THING YOU MAY NOT KNOW ABOUT ME

* Have participants stand in a circle.

- Ask each participant to say her name and complete the statement: "One thing you may not know about me is . . ."
- Model the statement first. Example: "One thing you may not know about me is I come from a big family" or "I have visited another country."

 ## ACTIVITY ONE :: SPECTROGRAM

- Have participants stand in the center of the room.
- Inform the group that one side of the room represents "Yes," the other side of the room represents "No," and the center of the room represents "Maybe."
- Explain that there is no talking or commenting during the exercise and that the participants should answer each question by moving to the "Yes," "No," or "Maybe" areas of the room.
- Explain that where you stand in each area symbolizes how strongly you hold that opinion.
- Using the **Sample HERstory Spectrogram Questions** sheet, ask ten to fifteen questions alternating between low-risk and high-risk. Feel free to adapt the questions to suit the needs of your group.
- After each question, ask the participants to observe, without comment, where they are in relationship to their classmates.

 ## PROCESSING QUESTIONS

1. *What happened in the exercise for you?*
2. *Did you like the opportunity to stand up for what you believe in without having to explain your position? Why or why not?*
3. *How did it feel to answer the questions without speaking?*
4. *Was there ever a moment when you stood alone? How did it feel?*
5. *Was there any question that you had an especially strong reaction to? Why?*
6. *Was there any time when you were surprised by who was near you? Why?*

 ## ACTIVITY TWO :: HUMAN BAROMETER

- Inform the participants that instead of asking questions, you are going to make statements and they are to answer in a similar way as they did during the Spectrogram activity.
- Explain that now the "Yes" end of the room is "Agree," the "No" end of the room is "Disagree," and the middle of the room is "Maybe/Unsure."
- Present the girls with a statement from the **HERstory Human Barometer Statements** sheet or with one you have created specifically for the group.
- Ask participants to respond nonverbally to the statement by moving to the appropriate area of the room.
- Once you have read the entire list of statements, ask the participants to return to their positions on the statement that generated the greatest diversity of responses.
- Distribute a piece of flip chart paper and a marker to the group of girls at each area.
- Instruct each group to discuss the statement and prepare a presentation of their position for the other groups.

- Have each group choose a spokeswoman to present the group's position.
- Remind the participants that when the spokeswoman is presenting, it is important that the other groups listen respectfully and not respond until it is their turn.
- After each group has presented its response to the statement, ask if anyone has been persuaded by the other groups' arguments. If so, have those participants join the group representing their new stance.
- *Option:* Give the groups a few minutes to prepare a rebuttal to the other groups' presentations. Have each spokeswoman present her group's case again, and if any of the girls are persuaded, they can move to a new group.

 ## PROCESSING QUESTIONS

1. *How do you feel right now?*
2. *Do you feel that others listened to you? If not, what got in the way?*
3. *How did it feel to give your opinion by "putting yourself on the line"?*
4. *How did you deal with people disagreeing with your position?*
5. *Did you move from one position on the line to another position? Why?*
6. *Where, in the world outside this group, do you have the opportunity to express your opinions?*
7. *Why is it important in those situations to articulate your thoughts?*
8. *Why is it important to listen to the other side of an issue and be open to changing your mind?*
9. *Where else in your life can you incorporate what you've learned today?*

 ## ACTIVITY THREE :: DIVERSITY PURSUIT

Segue: Diversity Discussion
- Have the participants sit in a circle.
- Ask the participants the following questions to open up the discussion:
    - What differences were revealed during the Spectrogram and Human Barometer activities?
    - Why are differences important?
    - What are some ways you can show that you accept someone's differences?
    - What does the word "diversity" mean?

Part 1: D.I.V.E.R.S.I.T.Y. Acronym
- Divide the girls into groups of four or five.
- Tell the participants that they will be working in their groups to create an acronym out of the word "diversity."
- Explain that an acronym is a word formed using the first letters of other words.
- Show the acronym example of the word "friends" to the class.
- Hand out one large piece of flip chart paper and markers to each group.
- Have the participants think about the word "diversity."
- Explain that participants will be describing "diversity" by using each letter of the word similarly to the F.R.I.E.N.D.S. acronym.
- Once all the groups have finished working, ask for volunteers to present their acronym to the class.
- Have groups share as time allows.

 **DISCUSSION QUESTIONS**

1. *What does "diversity" mean to you?*
2. *What are the benefits of diversity?*
3. *How does diversity relate to conflict?*

Part 2: Diversity Pursuit

- Have participants remain seated at their desks.
- Explain to the participants that they are going to play a game similar to bingo called Diversity Pursuit.
- Refer students to the **Diversity Pursuit** worksheet.
- Tell participants the object of this game is to fill up their sheets with other participants' names.
- Explain that participants will be walking around looking for a person for whom the statement in the box on the card is true. That person will then sign the box on the card. For example, if the box says, "Has more than three sisters," participants will walk around the room looking for another student who has more than three sisters to sign that box.
- Tell participants that they may not call out to find out who might be able to sign a box but instead must ask other participants directly.
- Tell the participants that they may sign each participant's card only once. (**Note:** If you have a small group, you may decide to allow participants to sign more than one box.)
- Allow participants to sign one of their own boxes, if an item is true for them (similar to a free space).
- Let participants know they should call out "Diversity" when they have filled their cards with signatures.
- When a participant calls out "Diversity," invite her to the front of the room so you can check her card. Instruct the other participants to keep playing.
- Continue the game until each participant fills up most of her card.

 **PROCESSING QUESTIONS**

1. *What happened?*
2. *Was it easy asking people about themselves? Why or why not?*
3. *What did you find out about other participants?*
4. *What was the best way for you to find out more information about others?*
5. *Why do you think we played Diversity Pursuit?*
6. *What are methods you can use to learn about other people outside the structure of this game?*

 **CLOSING :: WHIP-AROUND**

- How will you be able to use what you learned about your fellow HERstory members today to uphold the HERstory Code?

Sample HERstory Spectrogram Questions

1. Is it easy to be a young woman?

2. Do you feel that the people you are surrounded by at school understand what you are going through?

3. Do you feel that the people you are surrounded by at home understand what you are going through?

4. Do you think women have to look out for one another?

5. Can you think of three women you look up to?

6. Do young people get the same respect that adults do?

7. Do young people give the same respect that adults do?

8. Do you respect only people who respect you?

9. Is it more important to be kind than to be good-looking?

10. Does our society view men and women as equal?

11. Are women capable of performing the same tasks as men and doing the same jobs just as well as men?

12. Are men and women judged by different standards when it comes to what's appropriate in dating?

13. Do you believe that a woman will be president of the United States in your lifetime?

14. Do you think it is important to be able to express your opinion?

15. Do you believe what someone intended to do matters more than what she really did?

16. Do you respect people based on their actions?

17. Are you sometimes judged by your actions?

18. Are you influenced by styles you see on TV and in magazines?

19. Has another girl ever insulted the way you look?

20. Have you ever insulted the way another girl looks?

21. Is there a part of your body that you do not like?

22. Is there a part of your body that you are proud of?

23. Do you believe that challenges make you stronger?

24. Do you look forward to being a role model someday?

25. Do you believe that everyone has the potential to make a difference in the world?

26. Do you believe that everyone has the potential to make a difference in the world around them?

HERstory Human Barometer Statements

1. I never change my beliefs once they are established.
2. Life is hard.
3. Happiness is a choice.
4. School is important for success.
5. People can't be trusted.
6. Sometimes you have to fight; there is no other choice.
7. Gay couples should be allowed to marry in the United States.
8. Police are people like you and me who are just trying to do their job.
9. Television is a negative influence on young people.
10. Thirteen years old is too young to lose your virginity.
11. Kids need discipline and rules.
12. Students should be allowed to pray in school.
13. All people are created equal.
14. Your actions define who you are.
15. Your words define who you are.
16. The number one way to measure success is money.
17. Respect should be earned.
18. Power should be earned.
19. Making people proud is important to me.
20. We create our own destiny.

Diversity Pursuit

Has a family member with a disability	Has witnessed others being bullied because they were perceived as being different	Speaks more than one language	Listens to the same type of music you do	Believes that all people are created equal
Has more than one race or culture in her family	Has read a book about a group of people different from herself	Has assisted someone with a disability	Has a friend or family member in the military	Wears clothing unique to her culture
Has a close friend of the opposite gender	Has a name with religious or cultural significance	Has ever been treated differently because of the way she looks	Has spoken up when someone said "that's so gay," "that's retarded," or another offensive term	Has traveled to another country
Is an only child	Celebrates holidays that are different from yours	Has a Facebook friend in another country	Went to a religious school	Was born in another country
Has experienced discrimination	Has attended the Puerto Rican Day parade	Has volunteered at a homeless shelter or soup kitchen	Knows sign language	Doesn't judge people by their sexual orientation

The Ties That Bind

OBJECTIVE
Participants will understand that life is full of both positive and negative experiences for everyone, and will determine how to work together to face a challenge.

SUMMARY
Participants have a discussion about life's highs and lows and take part in interactive team-building activities.

AIM
How does better understanding one another affect the way a group works together to face a challenge?

STANDARDS
CCSS – RI.7, SL.1, SL.2, SL.4, L.1, L.6
SEL – Self-Awareness, Self-Management, Relationship Skills

MATERIALS
*flip chart paper; CD player or MP3 player with lively music; **My Life**, **Mountains and Valleys**, and **Your Many Roles** worksheets (pp. 5–7 in the Student Writing Companion); stopwatch (optional); colored cardstock for Cooperation Squares*

Lesson Vocabulary

cooperation n., the act of operating together for the common good

high adj., having a relatively great elevation; extending far upward; greater than usual or expected; favorable

low adj., lacking liveliness or good spirits; discouraged or dejected; below an average or a standard; depreciatory; disparaging

problem solving n., explaining, resolving, or finding a solution to what is difficult to be understood

ACTIVITY ONE :: MOUNTAINS AND VALLEYS

FACILITATOR NOTE
If your Opening Ritual for each day is Rose and Thorn, explain that this activity will be taking your ritual to a deeper level.

Part 1: Highs-and-Lows Mingle
- Write the Aim on flip chart paper and ask participants what they think "highs" and "lows" are.
- Review the Lesson Vocabulary.
- Ask participants to mingle around the room while you play music.
- Tell the group that when the music stops, everyone should find a partner.

- Stop the music.
- Once everyone is partnered, have participants answer the following question with their partner: "What is one of your 'highs,' or positive experiences, from this week?" Explain that each partner should answer the question.
- After a few minutes of discussion, turn the music back on and ask participants to mingle again. Explain that once the music stops, everyone should find a new partner.
- Stop the music again.
- Once participants have found their new partners, have them answer the following question: "What is one of your 'lows,' or negative experiences, from this week?" Remind them that each partner should share an answer.
- Continue with a few more rounds, asking participants to discuss their highs and lows from the past month or year, or from their lifetimes, with a new partner each time.

Part 2: My Highs and Lows
- Point participants to the **My Life** worksheet.
- Ask participants to create a "life map" using the structure of the worksheet to chart the mountains and valleys, or highs and lows, that they have experienced in their life so far.
- Share your own life map as an example.

 ## DISCUSSION QUESTIONS

1. *How did it feel to fill out the **My Life** worksheet?*
2. *Was it easy or difficult? Why?*
3. *Why is it important to reflect on our highs and lows?*
4. *What do we learn from reflecting on our experiences?*

Part 3: Mountains and Valleys Once Around
- Explain to participants that you will be giving them a second worksheet. On it there will be several boxes, and each box contains a sentence. Tell participants that each sentence describes situations that cover some of the highs and lows we experience in our lives.
- Point participants to the **Mountains and Valleys** worksheet.
- Explain that each participant should write her name at the top of her sheet, and that she should initial her worksheet in every box that describes an experience she has had at one time in her life.
- Tell participants that once they've initialed their own boxes, you are going to give them three minutes (or the length of one song) to mingle around the room with their worksheets and try to get as many signatures from other girls as they can before the allotted time is up.
- Explain that participants should initial the boxes of their classmates' worksheets that pertain to them, and that participants can sign more than one box on a worksheet.
- After the allotted time, ask participants to return to their seats and review their worksheets.

DISCUSSION QUESTIONS

1. *How did the experiences described in the boxes relate to your life map?*
2. *Were you surprised by how many participants have shared experiences?*
3. *What does this game tell us about our emotions and our experiences?*
4. *Why is it important that we share our highs and our lows with others?*
5. *Do you think there are any experiences people have that are completely unique to them, and no one else has ever experienced?*
6. *What would life be like if we had no lows?*

FACILITATOR NOTE

Tell participants that now that they have learned what challenging experiences they have had in common with one another, they are going to work together to overcome a common challenge in a game called Cooperation Squares.

ACTIVITY TWO :: COOPERATION SQUARES

Part 1: Cooperation Squares

- Divide the girls into groups of five participants.
- Place four pieces of paper per group on the floor in close proximity to the participants.
- Explain that the goal of the activity is for each member of each group to be touching a piece of paper.
- Tell participants that the only rule of the activity is that no one can be touching the floor. Demonstrate this by standing with both feet on a piece of the paper.
    Note: To encourage group problem solving, if a participant asks any question, such as, "Can we move the paper?" simply respond, "There is only one rule: No one can be touching the floor."
- Have groups begin the activity by trying to achieve the goal by whatever means possible.
- Tell participants to call you over if they think they have achieved the goal so you can inspect their position.
- Let participants know that they must hold their position for a count of ten.
- Once a group achieves the goal, increase the challenge by removing one sheet of paper at a time and having the group try to achieve the goal again. Repeat until the groups have successfully placed all members on top of the final square.
- Congratulate each group each time it succeeds.

FACILITATOR NOTE

The goal of this lesson is for participants to problem solve and feel the success of achieving the goal on their own. Do not offer ideas on how to go about this activity or prompt participants in any way. If the group is stuck, trust the process. The simple response "There is only one rule: No one can be touching the floor" is an effective way to encourage group problem solving.

PROCESSING QUESTIONS

1. *What happened in your group?*
2. *How did you feel?*
3. *How did your group work together?*
4. *How did you get your ideas?*
5. *What were some ways your group tried to solve the problem?*
6. *What happened when your group, or someone in it, got discouraged?*
7. *What happened when a strategy did not work?*
8. *Is there anywhere else in your life where you have had to solve a group challenge?*
9. *What are some key factors a group needs to be successful?*
10. *How can you use what you learned about cooperation within our HERstory community?*

Part 2: Your Many Roles

- Brainstorm with participants the different roles that emerged in the Cooperation Squares activity and write them on flip chart paper. For example, was there a leader in your group? A mastermind? A worker? A cheerleader?
- Point participants to the **Your Many Roles** worksheet.
- Instruct the participants to complete the worksheet. Tell them to write their name in the center circle of the page and then list the different roles that they play in their life in the outer circles.
- Tell participants that they can refer to the brainstorm list on the flip chart paper or come up with roles on their own.

PROCESSING QUESTIONS

1. *Was it easy or difficult to brainstorm all the roles you play in your life?*
2. *What surprised you about your many roles?*
3. *Why is it important to understand all the roles you play in your life?*
4. *What is a role you would like to play that you do not yet play?*

CLOSING :: WHIP-AROUND

- What would you like your role to be within the HERstory community?

My Life

Life is full of highs and lows. Sometimes we have mountains, and sometimes valleys.

Think about your life and what you consider to be your biggest highs and lows so far, then write about them in the space below.

MOUNTAINS	VALLEYS

Mountains and Valleys

Has ever won an award	Has ever lost a pet	Has ever made another person feel good about himself/herself	Has ever felt guilty	Has ever insulted someone
Has ever felt afraid	Has ever been broken up with by a boyfriend or girlfriend	Has ever done really well on an important test	Has ever felt excited about something	Has ever had a loved one pass away
Has ever been called a racial slur	Has ever been accused of something	Has ever felt alone	Has ever fallen in love	Has ever felt completely happy
Has ever been judged by someone	Has ever done well at a sport or hobby	Has ever been pleasantly surprised	Has ever discovered something new about herself	Has ever been given an unexpected gift
Has ever felt embarrassed	Has ever had something stolen	Has ever made a team or a program that she really wanted to be part of	Has ever made a mistake	Has ever been proud of herself

Your Many Roles

You

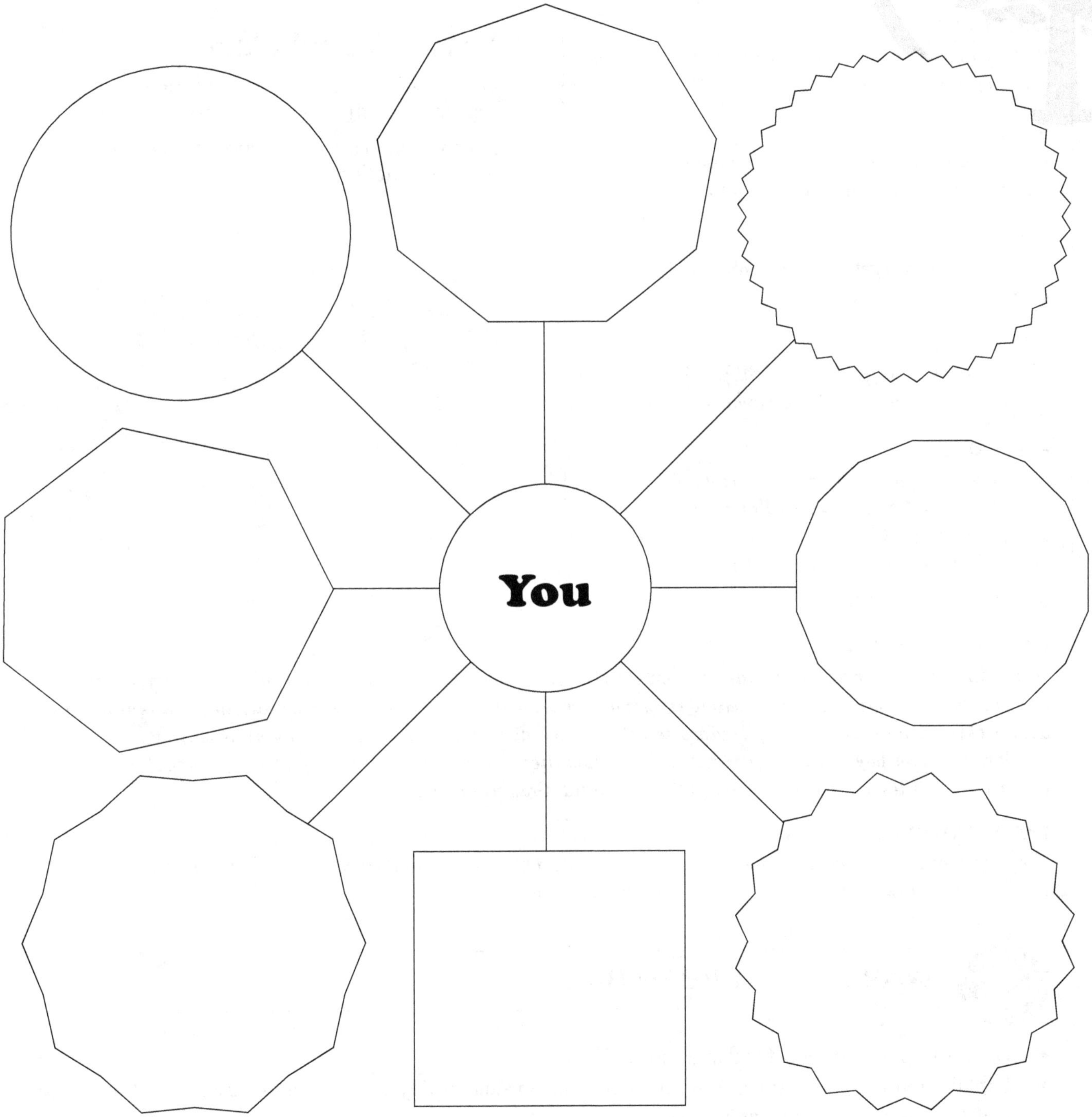

Lights, Camera, Action!

OBJECTIVE
Participants will demonstrate creative self-expression and cooperation skills.

SUMMARY
Participants will work together in groups to plan music videos and commercials with a twist.

AIM
How can we work together to create an artistic product?

STANDARDS
CCSS – RI.7, W.3, W.4, SL.1, SL.2, SL.4, L.6
SEL – Self-Awareness, Social Awareness

MATERIALS
sheet of 8½ x 11 paper to crumple, two sets of five or six index cards, **Get It While It's Hot!** *worksheet and* **Can't Use It? Just Sell It!** *handout (pp. 8–9 in the Student Writing Companion), and a few prop bags*

Lesson Vocabulary

cooperation n., the act of operating together for the common good

plan v., to have the will and intention to carry out some action

PREPARE IN ADVANCE
On the first set of five or six index cards, write one musical genre on each (e.g., hip-hop, rock 'n' roll, country, opera, R & B, jazz, blues, show tunes); on the second set of index cards, write two target audiences on each that are as different as possible (e.g., nuns and motorcycle gangs, teenagers and senior citizens, business executives and surfers, etc.).

Prepare a prop bag containing a variety of "unsellable items" to choose from: boas, funny hats, prop glasses, torn books, whistles that make no sound, silly wigs, Mardi Gras beads, etc.

FACILITATOR NOTE
The participants will be creating imaginary videos—you do not need an actual video camera for this lesson. However, if you have access to one, you can use it as an option.

 ## WARM-UP :: URBAN BALL

- Have the participants stand in a circle.
- Explain that they will be working on cooperation skills today, and the only way to win this game is if they work together as a team.
- Crumple a piece of paper into a ball and explain that the object of the game is for the group

to keep the ball in the air by hitting it with their hands fifteen times in a row. (You may want to increase or decrease the goal number depending on the proficiency of the group.)

- Go over the game's guidelines with the group:
  - The group counts together out loud each time the ball is hit. If the ball is missed and hits the floor, the count starts over.
  - The same person cannot hit the ball two times in a row. If someone does, the count starts over.

ACTIVITY ONE :: 1, 2, 3, VIDEO!

Segue: Remind participants that they have been working as a group to solve challenges, and tell them that today the challenges are going to be artistic.

- Have participants sit in a circle.
- Tell them that they are going to make imaginary music videos.
- Ask participants to warm up their voices. Lead the group in a few rounds of "Twinkle, Twinkle Little Star" until everyone feels comfortable with it. The lyrics are:

  > "Twinkle, twinkle little star,
  > how I wonder what you are.
  > Up above the world so high,
  > like a diamond in the sky.
  > Twinkle, twinkle little star,
  > how I wonder what you are."

Note: If a participant doesn't want to sing or is reluctant, she can join in later in other ways (e.g., as a dancer, stagehand, videographer).

- Tell the participants that they are going to make a series of music videos using different styles of music.
- Divide the class into groups of four or five and send them off to their "rehearsal space" in different corners of the room. Tell the class that they will perform their videos after rehearsal. Encourage participants to be as creative as possible.
- Assign music genres by having each group pick an index card.
- Let the participants know that they may use personal props for their videos.
- Give the groups approximately ten minutes to make their music videos in the selected genres, using "Twinkle, Twinkle Little Star" as their lyrics.
- When time is up, reassemble the groups and create an audience and a stage area. Invite each group to share its rendition of "Twinkle, Twinkle Little Star," beginning each video by calling out "1, 2, 3, video!" or "Lights, camera, action!"
- Encourage the audience to give thunderous applause after each video is performed.

Note: During the performances you may want to be the cameraperson and pretend to film the videos.

PROCESSING QUESTIONS

1. *What happened in this activity?*
2. *How did it feel to work together as a group? Was it easy/difficult?*
3. *What are some skills you used in this activity that could be helpful in other areas of your life?*
4. *Are you part of a group that is currently facing a challenge? If so, what is the group?*
5. *What is one strategy you will use to address that challenge?*

 **ACTIVITY TWO :: GET IT WHILE IT'S HOT!**

Segue: Ask participants if they are ready for the next challenge.

Part 1: Get It While It's Hot!
- Point participants to the **Get It While It's Hot!** worksheet.
- Divide participants into groups of five or six.
- Have participants collaborate to write a short newspaper ad for a hard-to-sell product. The ad should include its funniest feature and the reasons someone should buy it, as well as any illustrations they would like to include.
- Tell participants they can invent their own hard-to-sell products or use one of the following examples: a dead plant, sunglasses with no lenses, a book without words, a stereo system with no volume, a phone that doesn't ring, a lollipop with no taste, a mug with holes in it, a bucket with no bottom.
- When the groups have finished writing, invite them to share the ads with the rest of the class.

 **DISCUSSION QUESTIONS**

1. *What happened in your group this time?*
2. *What skills are necessary to create an ad for an unsellable product?*
3. *What were the benefits of working together?*
4. *What did your group do to work together successfully?*
5. *If there were disagreements in your group, what did you do to solve them?*

Part 2: Lights, Camera, Action!
- Tell participants to stay in their groups.
- Have each group review the **Can't Use It? Just Sell It!** instructions.
- Inform the participants that their task as a team is to create a television commercial for the hard-to-sell product they just wrote the ad for.
- Instruct the teams to come up with as many selling points as possible for their product and to include a demonstration on how to use it. Encourage them to be as creative as possible.
- Tell the groups that they have to promote this product to two separate target audiences. Explain that they should create two commercials, one for each target audience they have been given.
- Instruct a participant from each team to come up and select a target audience index card from a hat or bag.
- Give this participant one of the previously prepared hard-to-sell items (or another hard-to-sell item for which they can create a television commercial), a prop bag, flip chart paper, and markers.
- Explain that they may incorporate any of the items in the prop bag into their commercials and that they should be as creative as possible.
- Allow the participants an appropriate amount of time to work on their commercials.
- Invite each team to come up and share both of their commercials. When they have finished, ask the audience to state what the product was (if it hasn't yet been spelled out) and guess who the target audiences were.
- *Option:* Instead of allowing groups to present each commercial separately, instruct them that whenever you call out "Switch," they will have to change to their other target audience. Call

out "Switch" several times during their commercials, so the group must go back and forth between their two target audiences.

DISCUSSION QUESTIONS

1. *What happened in your group this time?*
2. *How did your team work together?*
3. *How did it feel to have a product (your commercial) at the end of your collaboration?*
4. *Are there any other places in your life where you have to switch tactics constantly?*
5. *Why is it important to be flexible when working together?*
6. *Name a time in the future that you might use skills you've practiced today in HERstory.*

CLOSING :: ELECTRICITY

- Ask the group to stand in a circle, hold hands, and close their eyes.
- Tell the group: "You are going to send a current of electricity around the circle by squeezing the person's hand on one side of you, who then passes on the squeeze in turn."
- Emphasize that the current can be whipped as fast as lightning if the group is concentrating and cooperating.

Get It While It's Hot!

Write an ad for a hard-to-sell product in the space below.

Be as creative and detailed as possible.

Can't Use It? Just Sell It!

Instructions

- Your task as a team is to create a commercial for a hard-to-sell product (e.g., a bucket with no bottom).

- Brainstorm as many selling points as possible about your product and include a demonstration of how to use it. Try to think of all the reasons why someone in your target audience should buy this product.

- Promote this hard-to-sell product to *two* separate target audiences (noted on your index card) by creating two different commercials, one for each target audience.

- Use as many props from your prop bag as possible in your commercials.

- Be as creative as you can!

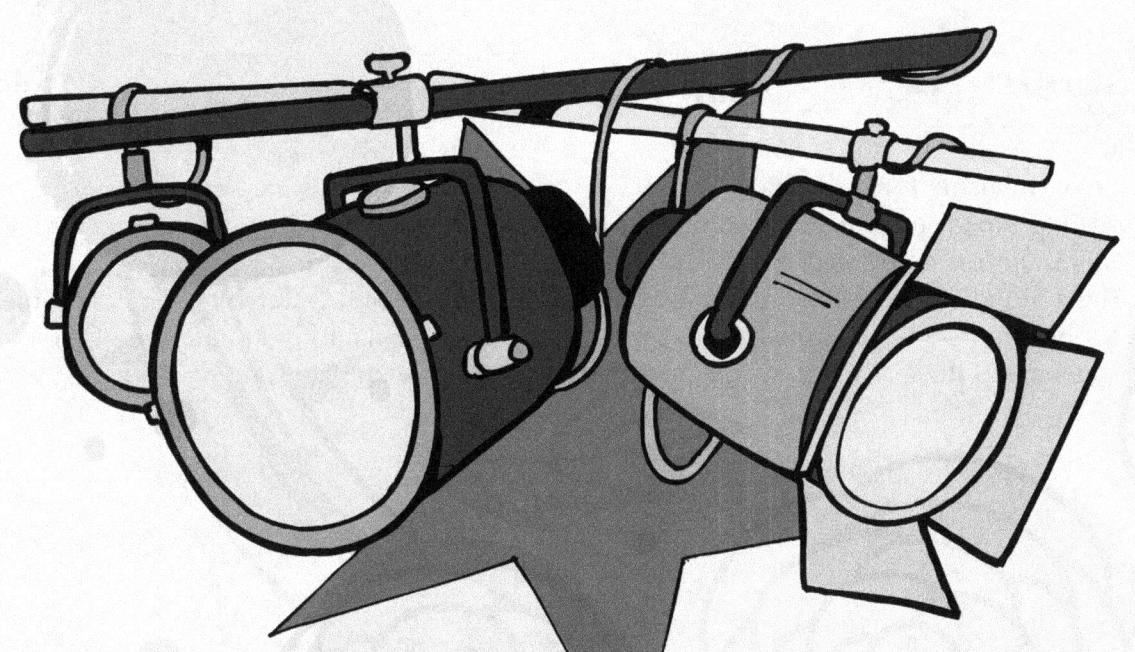

Introduction to Character

OBJECTIVE
Participants will define "leadership" and "character."

SUMMARY
Using of a variety of worksheets, participants define "character" and investigate the origins of one's character.

AIM
What is character, and where does my character come from?

STANDARDS
CCSS – RI.7, W.4, SL.1, SL.2, SL.4, L.6
SEL – Self-Awareness, Social Awareness, Relationship Skills

MATERIALS
Character Worksheet, Your Top Ten Character Qualities, Character Profile, Why I Am the Way I Am, and Personality Goes a Long Way worksheets (pp. 10–17 in the Student Writing Companion), flip chart paper, index cards with closing questions

Lesson Vocabulary

character n., the sum of internal qualities that make someone distinctive, especially someone's qualities of thought and feeling

composite n., a total made up of distinct parts

origin n., the point at which something comes into existence or from which it is derived

personality n., the overall pattern of collective character, behavioral, temperamental, emotional, and mental traits that are peculiar to a specific person

prioritize v., to rank; to create an order of importance

profile n., a representation of someone in outline

trait n., a distinguishing quality or peculiarity

PREPARE IN ADVANCE:
*Fill out a **Character Profile** worksheet to bring as an example. Then, prepare the discussion questions for Activity Three, Part 3, by writing out and numbering each question on separate index cards.*

WARM-UP :: POWER NAME

- Have participants form a circle.
- Explain to the group that you are going to get to know each other by creating "power names."
- Model the exercise by saying: "My name is _____, and I am _____."
- In the second space, use an adjective beginning with the first letter of your first name that describes yourself in a positive way (e.g., "My name is Carol and I am courageous.")
- Going around the circle, have each participant share her name and one positive quality about herself.

ACTIVITY ONE :: CHARACTER BRAINSTORM

Part 1: Character
- Write the word "character" on flip chart paper taped to the board.
- Ask participants what they think "character" means, and list their responses under the word.
- Read the Lesson Vocabulary definition of "character" to the group and add it to the list.
- Refer students to the **Character Worksheet**.
- Tell the participants to look at the boxes on the worksheet and circle the ones that they think represent someone who has character.
- Have them fill in the blank boxes with people of character they know in real life who are not on the worksheet.
- Choose some volunteers to read aloud their choices.
- Ask if anyone wrote down examples that were not on the worksheet, and request that they share their responses.

Part 2: Leadership
- Repeat the Lesson Vocabulary definition of "character" for the group.
- Have participants look at the boxes they chose on the worksheet and write down one quality that describes each person on the blank line.
- When everyone has finished, ask for volunteers to share their answers with the class.
- Write their answers on flip chart paper.
- Ask participants to define "leadership."
- Read the Lesson Vocabulary definition of "leadership" and add it to the flip chart paper.
- Tell participants to take one last look at their worksheet and put a checkmark by the people they think exemplify leadership.

DISCUSSION QUESTIONS

1. *Was the class definition of "character" different from or similar to the vocabulary definition? In what way?*
2. *Do these definitions affect how you see other people? Yourself? In what way?*
3. *What is the relationship between character and leadership?*

ACTIVITY TWO :: BIRDS OF A FEATHER

- Refer students to the **Your Top Ten Character Qualities** worksheet.
- Brainstorm character qualities with the class.
- As a group, narrow down these qualities to the top ten.
- Have participants copy these onto the worksheets.
- Give the participants five minutes to prioritize the qualities for themselves from most to least important.
- Have the group stand and spread out around the room.
- Explain that when the game begins, participants should speak only in whispers and try to get into pairs as fast as possible.
- For the first round, have participants look for another girl whose most important quality is the

same as theirs.
- Give the pairs a moment to share the reason behind their ranking.
- Repeat this process for the following two rounds:
  - Look for someone who has the same quality ranked in the middle (ranked third through sixth).
  - Look for someone whose lowest-ranked quality is highest on your own list.

 **PROCESSING QUESTIONS**

1. *What was it like to prioritize character qualities?*
2. *What was it like to share the character qualities that you consider the most important with someone else?*
3. *What was it like to hear someone else's most important character qualities?*
4. *In what interactions do people's character qualities have an important impact? Why?*
5. *How can you use what you learned about the importance of different character qualities in your life?*

 **ACTIVITY THREE :: CHARACTER PROFILE**

Part 1: Character Profile
- Tell participants: "Think of someone you know personally whose character has had a positive effect on your life."
- Refer students to the **Character Profile** worksheet.
- Have participants answer the questions on the worksheet for the person they have in mind.

 **DISCUSSION QUESTIONS**

1. *If more than one person came to mind, how did you decide whom to profile?*
2. *Would you add anything else to this sheet to make it a good description of your person's character? What?*
3. *How would this have been different if I had said, "Choose anyone" rather than "Choose someone you know personally"? Why?*

Part 2: Minute Share
- Have participants quickly get into pairs.
- Allow each pair to discuss their profiles, one minute per participant.
- If time allows, choose a pair or two to share their profiles with the group.

Part 3: Character Discussion
- Ask for five volunteers and hand them the prepared index cards.
- Going in the order of the numbered questions, have each volunteer read her question and solicit answers from the class.
- The questions on the cards are:
  1. Do you think anyone might choose you for this character profile? Why? Why not?

2. Do you consider yourself to be a person of character? Why? Why not?
3. How does character affect your life?
4. Why is talking about the idea of character important?
5. If you went out tomorrow and had a group of adults outside of this school do character profiles, what would happen that would be similar to what you did? What would be different?

Part 4: My Character Profile
- On the bottom of the **Character Profile** worksheet, have participants answer two of the questions about themselves.

DISCUSSION QUESTIONS

1. *Now that you have finished these activities, what character quality do you think is most important? Is it the same quality you ranked highest at the start of this session?*
2. *Where do you think character traits come from?*

ACTIVITY FOUR :: MY CHARACTER

Part 1: Why I Am the Way I Am
- Refer students to the **Why I Am the Way I Am** worksheet.
- Give the participants five minutes to complete Parts 1 and 2 of the worksheet.

DISCUSSION QUESTIONS

1. *What are some words you used to describe your personality or your character?*
2. *Where did some aspects of your personality come from (e.g., your sense of humor, your personal style)?*
3. *Where did some of your character traits come from (e.g., loyalty, honesty)?*
4. *Did you have more elements in the "Born with It" or the "Picked It Up" category?*
5. *What are some of your favorite personality or character traits?*
6. *What are some of your least favorite personality or character traits?*
7. *Has your personality/character changed over the years? For better or for worse?*

Part 2: It's Natural/It's Nurtured
- Ask the group to respond to the following three questions by a show of hands:
  1. Who thinks the traits you're born with are the most important in making you who you are?
  2. Who thinks that the traits you pick up are the most influential?
  3. Who thinks that personality and character are equally defined by what you're born with and what you pick up in life?
- Inform participants that they will now do a quick exercise that examines the origins of their personality and character.
- Divide the girls into three groups according to how they voted on the three questions.
- Distribute a piece of flip chart paper and a marker to each group.
- Tell each group to come up with five reasons to support its opinion of what has the greatest

influence on creating personality and character.

- Once the groups have completed their lists, have each one select a member to present the reasons they came up with.

 **DISCUSSION QUESTIONS**

1. *Did your thoughts on what defines personality or character change after hearing each group present its case? Why or why not?*
2. *How will you take these different aspects of personality and character traits into account when evaluating yourself?*
3. *How will you take these different aspects of personality and character traits into account when dealing with someone who is different from you?*

Part 3: Personality Goes a Long Way
- Have the students complete the **Personality Goes a Long Way** worksheet.

 **DISCUSSION QUESTIONS**

1. *Was it easier to think of personality/character traits that you like about yourself or that you dislike about yourself?*
2. *Where did the majority of the traits you like come from? The ones you dislike?*
3. *Why is it important to learn to accept yourself?*
4. *Why is it important to work to improve yourself?*

 **CLOSING :: WHIP-AROUND**

- Have participants complete the following statement: "One thing I learned about character today was . . ."

Character Worksheet

Grandmothers	Victor Cruz		Lil Wayne
	minister	Angelina Jolie	George W. Bush
Michelle Obama	Jay-Z	Hillary Clinton	teachers
	SpongeBob SquarePants	Venus and Serena Williams	Martin Luther King Jr.
Lady Gaga		Bill Gates	Barack Obama

Your Top Ten Character Qualities

List Your Qualities:

1.

2.

3.

4.

5.

6.

7.

8.

9.

10.

Reorganize Your List in Order of Importance to You:

1.

2.

3.

4.

5.

6.

7.

8.

9.

10.

Character Profile

A PERSON WHOSE CHARACTER HAS IMPRESSED YOU:

_____

(Answer the questions below according to what you know and what you would suppose about this person. *If you don't know, guess.*)

1. One quality of this person's character that has affected me:

2. One example of how that character quality affected me:

3. One thing this person has said that I can remember:

4. How do other people see this person? (*As a . . .*)

5. Who or what do I think shaped this person's character?

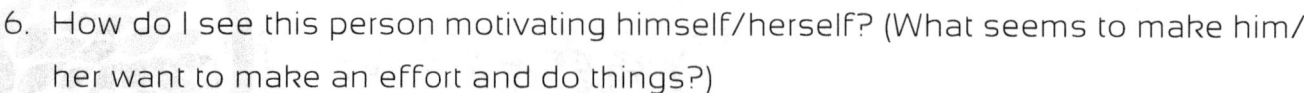

6. How do I see this person motivating himself/herself? (What seems to make him/her want to make an effort and do things?)

7. If there was one thing this person would want to pass on as his/her legacy to others, what do I think it would be?

8. What parts of the person's character have I seen him/her work to improve?

Choose two of the questions above and answer them *about yourself* in the two spaces below:

1.

2.

Why I Am the Way I Am

You are who you choose to be, but your personality—what makes you *you*—comes from traits you're born with and traits you've picked up from the world around you. Personality goes a long way. What's yours?

PART 1

In the space below, list some of the parts of your personality that are specific and peculiar to you (e.g., your sense of humor, the way your mind works, your sense of style).

PART 2

Looking at some of the traits you just wrote down, think about where these aspects of your personality and the character traits we discussed earlier may have come from.

In the space below, divide each of your personality and character traits into one of the following two categories: **Born with It** (e.g., traits your family gave you) and **Picked It Up** (e.g., what you've adopted from your neighborhood, your school, your community, television, movies, fashion).

THE WAY I AM

Born with It:

Picked It Up:

Personality Goes a Long Way

PART 1

Some personality or character traits you're born with. Some you pick up along the way. Fill in the columns below to rate the traits of your personality and character—which traits you like, which you wish you could change, and where you think they came from.

PERSONALITY/CHARACTER TRAITS I LIKE ABOUT MYSELF:	WHERE I THINK THEY CAME FROM:
1.	
2.	
3.	
4.	
5.	

PERSONALITY/CHARACTER TRAITS I WISH I COULD CHANGE ABOUT MYSELF:	WHERE I THINK THEY CAME FROM:
1.	
2.	
3.	
4.	
5.	

PART 2

1. How can you maintain the personality/character traits you like about yourself?

2. How can you change the personality/character traits you don't like about yourself?

Ethical Minds Want to Know

OBJECTIVE
Participants will define "ethics" and identify the ethics of various groups in their lives.

SUMMARY
Participants brainstorm ethics of various groups and focus on the ethics of groups to which they belong.

AIM
What are the ethics of groups to which I belong?

STANDARDS
CCSS – RI.1, RI.7, W.1, W.3, W.4, W.7, SL.1, SL.2, SL.4, L.6
SEL – Self-Awareness, Social Awareness

MATERIALS
*several sheets of blank flip chart paper; markers; tape; the **Ethical Case Study**, **Questionable Ethics**, and **Ethical Minds Want to Know** worksheets (pp.18–22 in the Student Writing Companion)*

Lesson Vocabulary

ethics n., the accepted system of principles or moral standards upheld by a group

WARM-UP :: ETHICS ISLAND

Part 1: Discussion: What Are Ethics?
- Use any or all of the following information and guiding questions to facilitate a discussion about ethics:
  - What are ethics?
  - How do the keywords "laws," "rules," "principles," and "standards" relate to ethics?
  - How do ethics affect a group?
  - What does it mean for a group to uphold an ethic? Can you give a specific example of this?
  - Comment on this statement by Rushworth M. Kidder: "Ethics is not a luxury or an option. It is essential to our survival." Do you agree or disagree? Why? How does the statement help us to understand ethics?
  - Comment on this statement, also by Kidder: "Culture by culture, people by people, there is a profound agreement that stealing is wrong." Do you agree or disagree? Why? Is the idea that stealing is wrong an ethic? How does the statement, particularly the words "profound agreement," help us to understand ethics?
- Point out to participants the difference between an established ethic (a rule or principle that

has been written down) and an undeclared ethic (a rule or principle that has not been formally written but is clearly understood by all).

- Share the following examples to further distinguish the two:
  - Established ethic: People in the workplace will not discriminate when hiring.
  - Undeclared ethic: Within a family, parents will treat all children equally.
- To conclude the discussion, ask participants to create a definition of "ethics."

Part 2: Ethics Island

- Break the participants into groups of three or four, and give each group a marker and a sheet of flip chart paper.
- Describe the following scenario to participants: Twenty people of various ages, cultural backgrounds, and economic statuses find themselves stranded on a desert island. The group agrees that to survive and live in peace, it must establish a set of rules, laws, or ethics that everyone agrees to live by.
- Have each group brainstorm a list of the top five rules, laws, or ethics that you feel these twenty people must establish to survive and live in peace.
- When the groups have completed their lists, have each one choose a spokeswoman to share its list.

Part 3: Follow-Up Brainstorm

- Create a "Global Ethics" brainstorm list on the flip chart paper.

DISCUSSION QUESTIONS

1. *What are examples of global (human) ethics that every person living in modern society is expected to live by? (Encourage students to refer to their responses from the Warm-Up.)*
2. *Why are these ethics necessary for survival?*

ACTIVITY :: ETHICAL MINDS WANT TO KNOW

Part 1: Case Study

- Help participants make the connection between ethics and groups. Explain that as humans we are a part of the large diverse group that is global society. This global society lives by a system of ethics, as we have discussed. Point out that smaller groups within our global society also have their own systems of ethics. Give the following examples:
  - Athletes: will not take drugs to enhance performance
  - Students: will not cheat on tests
  - Police: will not use unnecessary force
  - Offer other examples of groups (e.g., lawyers, doctors, gangs) and see if participants can identify one ethic that each group lives by.

Note: At this point you may want to address the fact that, of course, not every athlete, policeman, etcetera, upholds the ethics of his/her group. However, that doesn't change the fact that for every group listed there is still a system of ethics in place. Remember, it's what the group is expected to uphold, not necessarily what the individuals actually uphold.

- Refer students to the **Ethical Case Study** worksheet.
- Ask for volunteers to read the case study aloud, one paragraph per volunteer.

- When reading is complete, lead students in a discussion using the four questions following the case study.

Part 2: Questionable Ethics

Segue: Point out that, so far, participants have been identifying ethics of groups in society. In the next part of the activity, they will be identifying ethics of specific groups they are a part of in real life.

- Refer students to the **Questionable Ethics** worksheet.
- Depending on the needs of the group, have participants either process ethical dilemma scenarios as a group or write their answers individually and then share with the group.

Part 3: Ethical Minds Want to Know

- Refer students to the **Ethical Minds Want to Know** worksheet and explain the instructions.
    - First, tell participants to identify four groups to which they belong.
    - Next, have participants note some of the ethics of each of those four groups, and ask them to reflect and comment on those ethics.
- Have some volunteers share an ethic of one group to which they belong.

 **PROCESSING QUESTIONS**

1. *How did it feel to identify ethics of groups you are a part of?*
2. *Did you notice a similarity of ethics between groups that you are a part of and groups that other participants are a part of?*
3. *In general, how do group ethics affect a person's life?*
4. *What are some specific examples of how the ethics of a group that you are a part of affect your personal life?*

 **CLOSING :: WHIP-AROUND**

- What is a group that you are a part of, and what is one ethic that it upholds?

Ethical Case Study

Read the following case study and answer the questions that follow.

Several years ago, a librarian was working the reference desk at the public library in her community. The phone rang. The caller, a male, wanted some information on state laws concerning assault. The librarian asked several questions to clarify the nature of his inquiry. Then, in keeping with long-established library policy designed to keep phone lines from being tied up, she explained that she would call him back in a few minutes after researching his question. She took down his first name and phone number, and then hung up.

The librarian was just getting up to do the research when a man who had been sitting in the reading area within earshot of the reference desk approached her. Flashing a police detective's badge, he asked for the name and number of the caller. The reason: the conversation he had overheard led him to suspect that the caller was the perpetrator of an assault that had happened the night before in the community.

What should the librarian have done? On one hand, she was a member of the community. She felt very strongly about the need to maintain law and order. As a woman, she was particularly concerned that an attacker might be at large in the community. And as a citizen, she wanted to do whatever she could to reduce the possibility that he might strike again. After all, what if she refused to tell and another assault happened the following night?

On the other hand, she felt just as strongly that her professional code as a librarian required her to protect the confidentiality of *all* callers. She felt that free access to information was vital to the success of democracy, and that if people seeking information were being watched and categorized simply by the kinds of questions they asked, a police state was not far behind. The right of privacy, she felt, must extend to everyone. After all, what if this caller was simply a student writing a paper on assault laws for a civics class?

The choice the librarian faced was clearly a difficult one. It was right to support the community's quest for law and order. But it was also right to honor confidentiality, as her professional code required.

Ethical Case Study Questions

1. What two groups was the librarian a part of that defined her ethics?

2. What were those ethics?

3. Describe why the ethics are in conflict.

4. If you were in this situation, what would you do?

Questionable Ethics

Choose one of the following questions to answer. Explain why you would make your decision and include what ethics come into play in making your decision.

- Would you commit a crime and spend a year in maximum-security prison if it meant that when you got out you'd be guaranteed $1 million?

- You really want a new iPad. Would you take one from a friend who admitted that he broke into a house, beat up the owner, and stole the iPad last weekend?

- Would you lie under oath in a court of law and say you witnessed a cop beat up an African American man in your neighborhood? What you actually saw was the cop push the man, not beat him up. However, you feel that so many cops get away with brutality, so why not try to make this cop an example?

....

....

....

....

....

....

....

....

....

....

Ethical Minds Want to Know

Part One

What are four groups to which you belong?
Example: Sports team, family, religious congregation

1.	3.
2.	4.

Part Two

Fill in your four groups in the spaces provided at the top of each column. Write some of the ethics of that group in the boxes provided underneath. **Circle** the ethics that you feel are easy for you to follow. **Underline** the ethics that you feel are harder to follow.

Group:	Group:	Group:	Group:

Ethical Minds Want to Know

Part Three

Base all of your answers on the ethics that you identified on the previous page.

1. Which ethics are easy for you to follow?

2. Which ethics are harder for you to follow?

3. Are there any ethics you don't necessarily agree with but follow because you are a part of that group? Why?

4. How do the ethics of these groups affect who you are?

Personal Values Posters

OBJECTIVE
Participants will define "value" and identify their personal values.

SUMMARY
Participants create posters that reflect their personal values.

AIM
What are my personal values?

STANDARDS
CCSS – RI.1, RI.7, W.3, W.4, SL.1, SL.2, SL.4, L.6
SEL – Self-Awareness, Social Awareness

MATERIALS
*colored cardstock, markers, magazines, scissors, stickers, art supplies, glue, the **Match the Value** and **Value Wheel** worksheets (pp. 23–26 in the Student Writing Companion), **Match the Value Facilitator Key**, your own premade Personal Values Poster, prepared flip chart paper*

Lesson Vocabulary
value n., principle or standard; the accepted principle or standard of an individual

FACILITATOR NOTE
Write the following list of words, statements, and "mottos" that you will use in Part 1 of the Warm-Up on the flip chart paper before the session begins:

- *Loyalty*
- *Family is the most important thing.*
- *What goes around comes around.*
- *Honesty*
- *All you need is love.*

WARM-UP :: MATCH THE VALUE

Part 1: Discussion: What Is a Value?
- Use the following guiding questions to generate a group discussion about values:
  - What is a value?
  - What does it mean when someone says, "I live by a set of values"?
  - What does it mean when something is of value in your life?
  - How might a value guide a person's actions?

- Read the prepared list of mottos, statements, and words on the flip chart paper.
- Ask participants to describe how each reflects a personal value. Encourage students to give examples of how that value might be reflected in a person's actions.

Part 2: Match the Value
- Refer students to the **Match the Value** worksheet.
- Instruct participants to do their best to match the role model/leader with a value they live by.
- When participants have completed the worksheet, discuss the matches and review the correct answers.

Note: Refer to the **Match the Value Facilitator Key** for the correct matches.
- To conclude the discussion, ask participants to define "value" and write the definition on the board.

ACTIVITY :: PERSONAL VALUES POSTERS

Part 1: Value Wheel
- Point participants to the **Value Wheel** worksheet.
- Instruct them to complete both sides of the worksheet following the instructions.
- Tell participants that in Part 1 they are to prioritize each category (e.g., work, friends) by numbering each section of the wheel according to what is most important in their life (1 denotes the most important).
- Tell participants that in Part 2 they are to list their top four categories and create a personal value statement for each.
- Have participants share some of their personal value statements and their answers to Part 3 of the **Value Wheel** worksheet.

DISCUSSION QUESTIONS

1. *How did it feel to come up with specific statements that reflect the values you live by? Was it easy or difficult?*
2. *Why is it important to be able to prioritize what you value most?*

Part 2: Personal Values Poster
- Hand out a piece of colored cardstock and markers to each participant.
- Explain to participants that they are to create at least five statements that express the personal values that they live by.
- Tell participants that their responses from the **Value Wheels** worksheet might help in creating these statements. If they choose, they can use the exact statements from the worksheet for their posters. They can also change their statements or write new ones.
- Instruct them to use their creativity to design a personal values poster that includes their five written personal value statements and any drawings, designs, symbols, images cut out from magazines, colorful artwork, or graffiti that they choose to add.

FACILITATOR NOTE
Model your own poster for the group and encourage students to use abstract as well as literal imagery. Let participants know that these posters can be used in the design of their set or can be included in their Literary Journal.

- When participants have completed their posters, have them share their work with the class.

PROCESSING QUESTIONS

1. *How did it feel to create a personal values poster?*
2. *What did you notice about other people's posters? Were there similarities in people's personal values?*
3. *Why is it important to be able to identify your personal values?*
4. *How do people express their personal values?*
5. *What are some specific examples of how your personal values affect your life?*

CLOSING :: WHIP-AROUND

- What is the most important personal value that you live by?

MATCH THE VALUE :: FACILITATOR KEY

The following are the closest matches for each leader and one value he or she live(d) by.

Note: Some of the answers to this worksheet may be interchangeable. This key is "correct" in that it denotes an applicable match for each. However, if participants come up with different logical matches, encourage their opinions.

- Nelson Mandela: "Any man or institution that tries to rob me of my dignity will lose."
- Gandhi: Nonviolence
- Jackie Robinson: Turn the other cheek
- Mother Teresa: Love and service
- Martin Luther King Jr.: Equality
- Muhammad Ali: "I'm free to be me!"
- Malcolm X: "By any means necessary."

Match the Value

Connect the leader with one value he or she lives/lived by.

Nelson Mandela   Nonviolence

Gandhi   "Any man or institution that tries
                              to rob me of my dignity will lose."

Jackie Robinson   "By any means necessary."

Mother Teresa   Equality

Martin Luther King Jr.   "I'm free to be *me*!"

Muhammad Ali   Love and service

Malcolm X   Turn the other cheek

Value Wheel

Part One

Prioritize each category by numbering each section of the wheel according to what you value most in your life (1 denotes the most important).

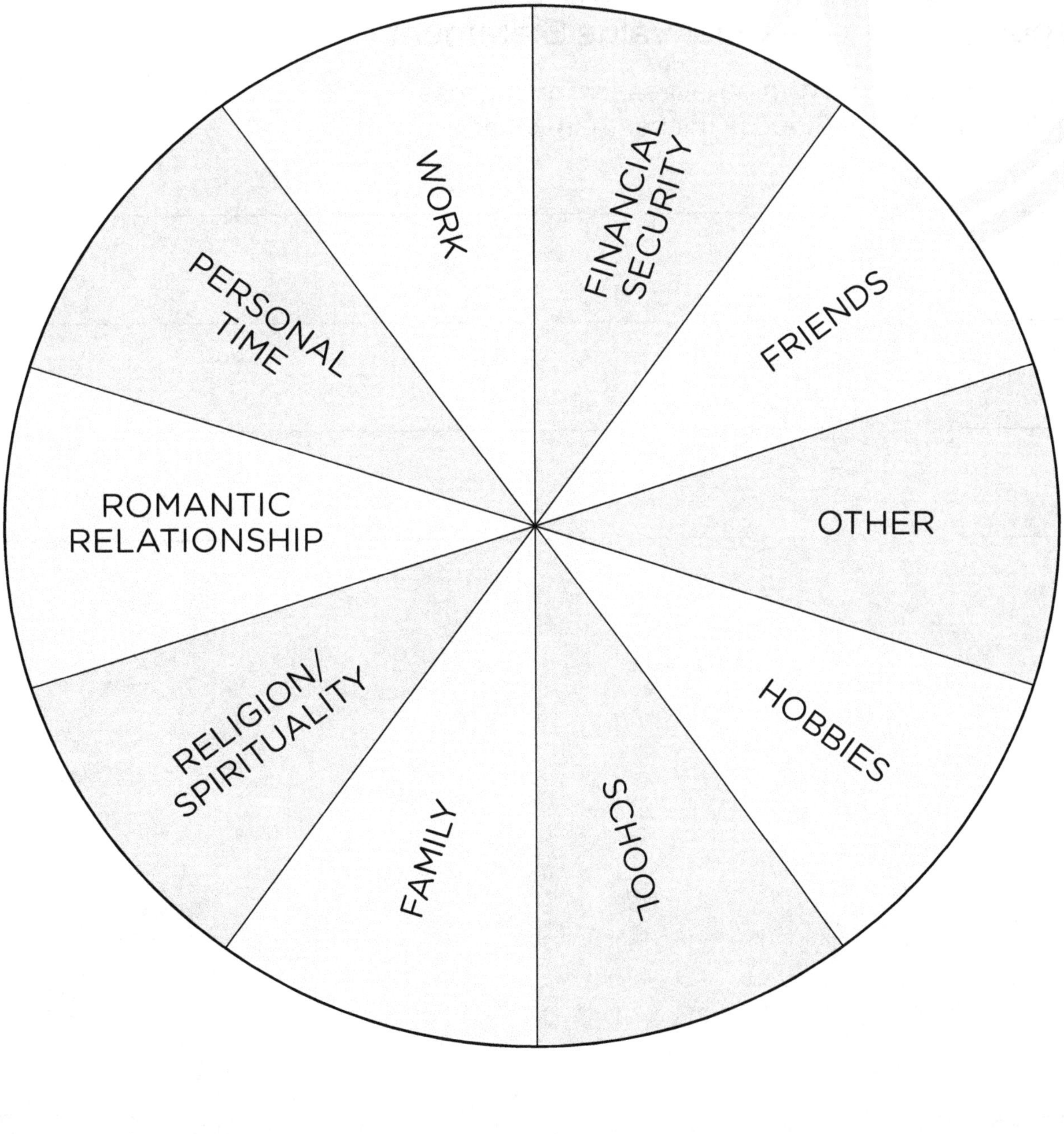

WORK

FINANCIAL SECURITY

PERSONAL TIME

FRIENDS

ROMANTIC RELATIONSHIP

OTHER

RELIGION/ SPIRITUALITY

HOBBIES

FAMILY

SCHOOL

Value Wheel

Part Two

List the top four categories that you value most from your wheel. Think about why each category is a priority in your life and what about it is most important to you. For each category create a personal value statement.

Category	Personal Value Statement
Example: Work	Work is necessary for success.
Example: Family	Blood is thicker than water.

1._____   _____

2._____   _____

3._____   _____

4._____   _____

NAME

Value Wheel

Part Three

Answer the following questions.

1. If you became famous, what is one thing you'd want the world to know about the "real" you?

....

....

....

....

2. If you were to write your future grandchild a letter, what would you tell him/her is one of the most important things to know in life?

....

....

....

....

3. Who is someone whom you consider a personal role model? What is one value that he/she lives by that is also important to you?

....

....

....

....

Choices, Decisions, Consequences

OBJECTIVE

Participants will define and analyze choices, decisions, and consequences.

SUMMARY

Through brainstorming, role-playing and decision-making practice, participants will understand potential consequences of choices.

AIM

What is the connection between choices, decisions, and consequences?

STANDARDS

CCSS – RI.7, W.3, W.4, SL.1, SL.2, SL.4, L.6
SEL – Self-Awareness, Social Awareness, Responsible Decision Making

MATERIALS

*Choices, Decisions, Consequences Sample Model; Choices, Decisions, Consequences: Setting the Scene; Choices, Decisions, Consequences Role Play; and **Decisions** worksheets (pp. 27–30 in the Student Writing Companion), flip chart paper, and markers*

Lesson Vocabulary

choice n., one of multiple options to select from

connection n., the relationship between things or events

consequence n., something that logically or naturally follows from an action; an effect

decision n., the act of reaching a conclusion or making up one's mind

WARM-UP :: ACROSS THE ROOM

- Ask participants to stand up and create two lines facing each other on opposite sides of the room.
- Tell participants you are going to make a series of statements. If the statement is true for the student she should cross to the other side of the room.
- **Note:** It does not matter which side students are on. The important thing is that students are moving when something is true for them.
- Begin each statement with "Cross the room if _____." Examples: "Cross the room if you are an only child," "Cross the room if you live in this neighborhood," "Cross the room if you like Chinese food."

FACILITATOR NOTE

You can use the questions that were not chosen for the Human Spectrum activities or create new ones along the same lines.

ACTIVITY :: CHOICES, DECISIONS, CONSEQUENCES

Part 1: Defining Choices, Decisions, Consequences

- Write the words "choices," "decisions," and "consequences" on flip chart paper.
- Solicit from participants the meaning of the word "choices." Write the suggestions next to the word.
- Ask for the meaning of the word "decisions." Write the suggestions next to the word.
- Repeat the process for the word "consequences."
- Read the Lesson Vocabulary definitions of the words, and ask participants to compare the brainstormed definitions and the Lesson Vocabulary definitions.

Part 2: Discussion

- Tell participants: "Each day we have choices available to us."
- Write the word "Situation" on the top left side of the flip chart paper.
- Write the words "Choices," "Decisions," and "Consequences" on the flip chart paper in three columns. See **Choices, Decisions, Consequences Sample Model** for the setup.
- Ask participants about a situation in which they have choices, decisions, and consequences.
- Write the participants' suggestions next to the word "Situation."
- Ask participants: "What are the choices in this situation?"
- Under "Choices," list all choices they call out. With participants, select one of the choices and write that choice under the "Decisions" heading.
- Brainstorm possible consequences to that decision and write several consequences under the "Consequences" heading.
- Repeat this process for each of the choices listed.
- Briefly discuss whether the consequence has a negative or a positive impact.

Part 3: Modeling Improvisation

- Tell participants they are going to create improvised scenes of a situation using choices, decisions, and consequences.
- Inform participants that to "improvise" means to create a scene that is not scripted or written out.
- Write a new situation on the flip chart paper (e.g., Your friends are staying out in the park past your curfew. You want to hang out with them, but your mom wants you home).
- Ask participants what choices are available for the situation.
- Ask for a volunteer to help you model an improvised scene.
- Tell participants to watch carefully as you improvise.
- Enact part one (the decision) of the scene. Freeze the scene after a character makes the decision.
- Ask the group what they saw in the scene, including the choices and decision made by the characters.
- Enact part two (the consequence) of the scene. Freeze the scene after the consequence is clear.
- Ask participants what the consequence was.

Part 4: Preparing Improvisations

- Divide participants into groups of four or five.
- Refer students to the **Choices, Decisions, Consequences Role Play** worksheet.
- In their groups, have participants create a situation and prepare an improvisation depicting the decision made.

- Next, have the groups prepare an improvisation depicting one consequence of that decision.
- Remind participants that to create a scene, they must decide who will be in it, where it will take place, and what should happen in the scene.
- Have students fill out the **Choices, Decisions, Consequences: Setting the Scene** worksheet.

Note: Even though participants are working in groups, they need to create improvisations with only two characters. Other members of the group can offer direction and record information onto the handout.

Part 5: Presenting Improvisations
- Ask participants to sit in the circle with their groups.
- Request volunteers to perform their scenes.
- Tell volunteers they will read the situation to the class first. Then, they will act out the scene, freezing after the decision is made. Finally, they will continue the scene until they act out the consequence.
- The audience should give volunteers a "One, two, three—action!" to begin. Have participants in the volunteer group read the situation to the class. Next, have performers enact the decision, then freeze. After that, performers enact the consequence, then freeze.
- Since they will be working without scripts, encourage participants to keep the dialogue going as best they can and to use their imaginations to improvise.
- Remind the participants that it is very important for the audience to remain silent. No calling out or disrupting the scene, especially when the scene escalates.
- Give actors a brief round of applause after each scene to support the participants who took a risk and volunteered.
- Ask the audience if the consequence was positive or negative. Why?
- If time permits, continue this process until all the groups have the chance to share.

FACILITATOR NOTE

Depending on the needs of your group, you may also have the girls freeze just before the pivotal decision is to be made and ask the audience to assist the actor in the decision making.

 ## PROCESSING QUESTIONS

1. *What happened?*
2. *How did you feel about creating scenes or improvisations?*
3. *How did your group decide who would do what in the activity?*
4. *What do choices, decisions, and consequences have to do with the real world?*
5. *When can you use this information in your life?*

Part 6: Real-Life Decisions
- Using the **Decisions** worksheet, ask students to write out a real-life situation involving an important decision they have to make.

 ## DISCUSSION QUESTIONS

1. *Why is it important to explore choices in a given situation?*

2. *Why is it important to imagine the consequence of a decision before making that decision?*

 **CLOSING ::** CURTAIN CALL

- Ask the volunteers who performed to stand and have everyone give them a round of applause.

Choices, Decisions, Consequences

Sample Model

Situation: Friends tell you another student has been spreading terrible rumors about you.

Choices	Decisions	Consequences
• Fight • Ignore it • Spread rumors about him or her • Tell a teacher	Fight	• Get hurt • Suspension • Props for being tough
	Ignore it	• Rumors stop • Rumors get worse • Stay in school
	Spread rumors about him or her	• Hurt feelings • Physical violence • Suspension
	Tell a teacher	• Teacher helps stop the rumors • Kids call you a snitch • Your parents find out

Choices, Decisions, Consequences

Setting the Scene

Answer the following questions and write out a situation that can be enacted in class.

Who are the characters in the scene?

Character A:

Character B:

Where will the characters be in the scene?

....

....

....

....

What is the situation?

....

....

....

....

....

....

....

....

Choices, Decisions, Consequences

Role Play

1. Decide what the situation is.
2. Decide who the characters will be.
3. Decide where the scene will take place.
4. List all the choices, decisions, and consequences.
5. Select one decision to be enacted, and circle it.
6. Select one consequence to be enacted, and circle it.
7. Decide who will play character A and character B in the scene. Only two people should be acting in the scene. The others in the group may introduce the scene, direct it, freeze it, etcetera.
8. Rehearse the scene.

1. Situation:

2. Character A: Character B:

3. Where will the scene take place?

4.

Choices	Decisions	Consequences

Decisions

Select a real-life situation in which you have to make an important decision. Complete the choices, decisions, and consequences portion of the chart.

Situation:

....

....

....

....

....

....

....

Choices	Decisions	Consequences

Free Your Voice

OBJECTIVE

Participants will articulate the benefits of cooperation in creating a forum for their individual and collective voice.

SUMMARY

Participants will work together to address group problems during a fast-paced team-building game. They will also watch the movie Freedom Writers *and answer related questions regarding the potential power of collective voices.*

AIM

Why is it important for a group to have a voice?

STANDARDS

CCSS – RI.7, W.3, W.4, W.6, W.7, SL.1, SL.2, SL.4, L.6
SEL – Self-Awareness, Social Awareness

MATERIALS

masking tape, thirty to thirty-five pieces of cardstock, markers, copy of Freedom Writers *DVD, the* **Movie Response Questions: Freedom Writers** *(pp. 31–32 in the Student Writing Companion)*

Lesson Vocabulary

challenge n., a test of one's abilities in a demanding but stimulating undertaking

cooperate v., to operate together for the common good

objective n., something worked toward or striven for; a goal

CLASSROOM SETUP

You will need a long, wide corridor of space in the classroom for the Warm-Up and Activity One. In preparation, place a line of tape on the floor at one end of the corridor, indicating where the "river" begins, and another line at the other end, indicating where it stops.

 ## WARM-UP :: WHERE DO I BELONG?

- Tell participants: "Today you will be working on cooperating with one another."
- Break students into two groups.
- Tell the groups to work together to order themselves alphabetically based on their first names as quickly as possible.
- If time allows, have them form other lines, such as by height, hair length, birth date, number of people in their household, minutes it takes them to get to school in the morning, etcetera.
- *Option:* Conduct the same exercise in silence.

PROCESSING QUESTIONS

1. *What happened?*
2. *How did it feel?*
3. *What happened in your groups?*
4. *If you faced challenges as a group, what strategies did you employ to overcome them? Where else might you be able to use these skills?*

ACTIVITY ONE :: STEPPING-STONES

Part 1: The River Challenge

- Hand out a piece of cardstock and a marker to each participant.
- Quickly brainstorm with the group the benefits of working with others to get something done (e.g., it's fun, it gets done faster, the outcome is better, diversity).
- Now ask the participants to write a word, phrase, or sentence on their piece of cardstock that describes what they think is the biggest benefit of working together.
- Collect the markers, but have the participants hold on to their cardstock.
- Ask the participants to stand up.
- Tell the participants there is a fast-flowing river that runs down the middle of the classroom. Explain that it is impossible to walk or swim through it, and that the only way to get across is by walking on stepping-stones (the pieces of cardstock in their hands).
- Tell them that the objective is for the entire group to get successfully across the river using only the stones they have.
- Explain that a part of someone's body must always be touching a stepping-stone or she will be swept away by the river.
- Demonstrate this for the participants.
- **Note:** When a stepping-stone is placed in the river, a foot must step on it immediately. Let the participants know that if no one is touching a certain stone, it will be swept away in the current—even one second without a foot on a stone is too long. (If a stone does not have someone touching it, you should snatch it up.)
- Have all participants stand with their cards (stones) behind the starting line.
- Allow participants two minutes to strategize.
- Instruct the group to begin. Monitor the group, taking away stones as necessary. As you take away a stone, read aloud the word, phrase, or sentence written on it. Ask the participants what they will do without that element.
- Stop the activity when the entire group gets across or when they run out of stones. Time permitting, you can allow an unsuccessful group to try again.

PROCESSING QUESTIONS

1. *What happened?*
2. *How did it feel to have a stone taken away? How did it feel to get/not get across?*
3. *How did your group work together? Was each individual's opinion respected and heard?*
4. *What strategies did you use to achieve your objective?*
5. *What rivers are you currently facing?*

6. *What stones are within our reach to surmount the obstacle that your "river" is presenting?*

 ## ACTIVITY TWO :: SCREENING OF FREEDOM WRITERS

- Show as much of Freedom Writers as time allows during this session. Show the remaining portion during the next session.
- Refer students to the **Movie Response Questions: Freedom Writers** worksheet before starting the film so that the students can keep the questions in mind as they watch.
- At the point at which you have to shut off the movie (before its conclusion) and close the club for the day, process whichever worksheet questions are applicable so far.

 ## CLOSING :: WHIP-AROUND

- If only part of the movie has been screened: What scene of the movie have you been most affected by so far?
- If the entire movie has been screened: What is one reason it is important for you to tell your story?

 ## ACTIVITY TWO (CONTINUED)

- Resume screening Freedom Writers. Based on the needs of your group, pause the film and process any teachable moments as needed.
- When the movie is over, allow participants time to answer the **Movie Response Questions: Freedom Writers** worksheet.
- Discuss and process the responses as a group.

 ## DISCUSSION QUESTIONS

1. *Why might we have shown this film on our final day before we begin our Writing Workshop?*
2. *What skills did these students learn from working as a team?*
3. *How did they use these skills to ensure their voices were heard?*
4. *In what ways were these students able to free their voices?*
5. *Why is it important to work as a group to free our own voices?*

 ## CLOSING :: WHIP-AROUND

- What is one reason why it is important for you to tell your story?

Movie Response Questions

Freedom Writers

DATE:

1. Why do you think the students in *Freedom Writers* decided to tell their stories?

2. How did it feel to hear these students tell their stories?

3. Do you like to write about things that you think/feel? If so, why? If not, why not?

4. Why is it important to write about your experiences and feelings?

5. What kinds of things can we learn by reading other people's stories?

6. What would you like to teach people through writing your own story?

Part Two
Writing Workshop

"Your writing voice is the deepest possible reflection of who you are."
—*Meg Rosoff*

"Do not follow where the path may lead. Go instead where there is no path and leave a trail."
—*Muriel Strode*

Writing Workshop

Section Guide

Material generated during the Writing Workshop will provide the text that you input into the HERstory Script Template (provided in the Reference section) to create your Ethnographic Theater Piece, or the text that you will compile for publication of your Literary Journal. For the participants to produce effective, honest, and evocative writing, they must be working in a well-established, creatively nurturing, and emotionally safe environment. This is best achieved by completing the entire Community Building section of HERstory before beginning the writing.

The Writing Workshop section is the first part of the curriculum to explicitly introduce the seven themes of HERstory:
- Identity
- Those You Are Closest To
- Body Image
- Love and Relationships
- Dreams
- Heritage or Tradition
- Legacy

These aspects of a young woman's experience will be the guiding themes for your Literary Journal or Ethnographic Theater Piece. The three types of lesson activities devoted to each theme in this section are:
1. a traditional lesson that is constructed to inspire exploration of and dialogue about the specific theme
2. Writing Prompts designed to allow participants the chance to express their beliefs about the theme
3. a suggested film and accompanying **Movie Response Questions** worksheet that can be used as a differentiated tool to provoke further dialogue

For organizational purposes, we have structured each lesson in this section to include three types of writing activities. Please be aware that these are extensive writing activities, and each theme will need a minimum of two to three sessions.

YOUR PARTICIPANTS

Supporting Various Skill Levels: Within your group, participants will have a range of learning styles, cognitive abilities, and basic writing skills. As a facilitator, you must gauge their abilities and adapt your discussion of the prompts accordingly. For example, ample time should be devoted to discussing metaphor if the group is not yet comfortable with using metaphor in their writing. The conversation should highlight not just the definition of "metaphor" but also the processing of why we might want to use structures such as metaphors within our Performance Piece or Literary Journal.

Individual Attention: It is essential to work with participants individually as they are writing to encourage them to use styles that not only highlight their strengths but also push the boundaries of what they assume they are capable of creating. For example, a girl who feels she struggles with poetry needs the attention and time of the facilitator and the help of her peers to become more comfortable with and expressive within the genre.

YOUR FACILITATION

Writing Style: It is very important to discuss at length with your group the style of writing that you are hoping to elicit from them. In general, the more figurative their language and the more abstract their imagery, the easier it will be to format into the script or journal structure. Participants should be encouraged whenever possible to answer in the form of a poem, a short story, etcetera. If you are in a school environment, do not hesitate to reach out to their English Language Arts teachers to assess what structures they are currently studying in class and to incorporate those structures into their HERstory writing if appropriate. For instance, if the girls are studying Shakespeare's sonnets, they can write a prompt response in the form of a sonnet; if they are studying haikus, they can respond in the form of a haiku.

Steering Toward the Final Project: If you are taking the Literary Journal track, you may adapt at your discretion the suggested ways in which the students write their answers (e.g., different style of poetry) based on the aesthetic you are choosing and the parameters that you are endeavoring to set for your journal. For the Performance Piece, it will be useful to allow the participants to answer in several different formats, as there is room within the structure of the script for everything from full poems to lists of words to extracted phrases.

YOUR SPACE

Adjusting the Space for Writing: It is equally as important to tend to your space during the Writing Workshop section as it is during Community Building. We recommend that many aspects of the space remain the same (e.g., posting the HERstory Code, playing music upon entry). However, you will also need to make adjustments to the space to make it an environment conducive to the students generating their writing responses. These adjustments might include altering the configuration of the chairs and desks, changing lighting levels, dedicating one area of the room solely for writing, etcetera.

Music: Depending on the character of your group, assess the need for additional environmental adjustments. For example, if your group is highly responsive to music, then generating a playlist for each of your writing days/themes is highly recommended. Taking a measured amount of participant suggestions for these playlists can initiate useful dialogue that may also lead to soundtrack choices for your Performance Piece.

Maintaining Rituals: Ensure that you maintain any rituals of respect for your space that you have established during the Community Building portion of the residency.

YOUR CURRICULUM

Curriculum Structure: Each theme includes a Leadership Program lesson to be facilitated as the first component. These lessons should be facilitated in the same manner as the lessons in the Community Building section, including the completion of accompanying worksheets, art projects, processing discussions, etcetera. Please note that excerpts of responses to several of these worksheets (e.g., **Who's the Woman?**) can be included in the Performance Piece or the Literary Journal.

Lesson Structure: The lessons in the Writing Workshop section are constructed so that the students may begin their writing during the second half of the visit in which they receive the curriculum lesson and continue their writing for a full session the next time the club meets. This second session of writing may also incorporate the screening of one of the recommended movies (see Suggested Films on the following page).

Writing Workshop Pages: Writing Workshop sections should be assigned and completed only after the participants have experienced the accompanying lesson. Do not assign participants writing workshop sections to complete if they have not yet participated in a theme's corresponding lesson.

Writing Prompts Completion: All the questions in the individual Writing Workshop lessons and the Writing Prompts relate to a corresponding part of the script template, or can be used as different approaches to a theme for the journal. It is, therefore, imperative that the students are encouraged to complete all of the Writing Prompts. It also is plausible that an answer to a question regarding one theme may be useful to apply to another thematic portion of the script (e.g., a participant's response in the Identity section may prove a good fit for a segment of the Legacy section).

Suggested Films: The recommended films can serve several purposes. First, they may appeal to participants of different learning styles and promote further, deeper dialogue on a theme. Second, they may be used on the second day of writing as a device to engage students who have finished their Writing Prompts section and to inspire the students who are still working. Included in the curriculum are **Movie Response Questions** worksheets for each of the films that correspond to a thematic section. These worksheets are designed to assist with focus and processing and to bridge the links between the movie's plotline and the theme of the current section.

Following are recommended films that have an accompanying **Movie Response Questions** worksheet:

- Identity: *13 Going On 30*
- Those You Are Closest To: *The Sisterhood of the Traveling Pants*
- Body Image: *Real Women Have Curves*
- Love and Relationships: *Enchanted*
- Dreams: *Take the Lead*
- Heritage or Tradition: *The Great Debaters*
- Legacy: *Pay It Forward*

Alternative Films and Corresponding Movie Response Questions worksheets: As new movies are constantly being produced and the needs of certain groups may vary, the recommended list here should not be considered mandatory or comprehensive. Feel free to select your own film for any of the thematic sections. However, if you do select your own film, it is important to generate your own **Movie Response Questions** worksheet for the purposes mentioned earlier. When creating this worksheet, keep in mind that the goal is not to review plot but to investigate aspects of the film that highlight the corresponding HERstory theme. Questions should focus on the context and perspective in which the theme is shown in the film, on how the participants' experience in their own lives relates to the characters' experiences, and what message the film sends about our society's view of women's experiences in relation to this theme.

Who's the Woman?

OBJECTIVE
Participants will articulate the qualities and characteristics of being a woman in today's society.

SUMMARY
Participants define their own ideas on being a woman by filling out a worksheet and playing an interactive game.

AIM
What does it mean to be a "woman"?

STANDARDS
CCSS – RL.1, RI.7, W.3, W.4, W.7, SL.1, SL.2, SL.4, L.6
SEL – Self-Awareness, Social Awareness

MATERIALS
__Who's the Woman?__ and __Lyric Breakdown__ worksheets, __Identity__ writing prompts, __Poem__ templates, copy of 13 Going On 30 DVD, and __Movie Response Questions: 13 Going On 30__ (pp. 34–46 in the Student Writing Companion), flip chart paper, markers

Lesson Vocabulary

expectation n., a standard of conduct or performance demanded by or of somebody

forbidden adj., not permitted; not allowed by order of somebody or by law

woman n., an adult female human being

PREPARE IN ADVANCE
Before the lesson, find lyrics to songs that are meaningful to young women exploring their identity and print copies of the lyrics. You may use selections from popular artists and songs that are meaningful to your group of girls, but be sure to vet all the lyrics to avoid inappropriate language. Some suggested songs to use include:

> *"Ladies First" by Queen Latifah featuring Monie Love*
> *"Independent" by Salt-N-Pepa*
> *"I'm Every Woman" by Chaka Kahn*
> *"All Hail the Queen" by Queen Latifah*
> *"I Used to Love Him" by Lauryn Hill*

Draw three large circles in the center of the flip chart paper and write one of the following in each: "The Woman," "Expected," and "Forbidden."

FACILITATOR NOTE
This lesson is substantial and may take a full session. If you finish the first two activities before the end of the first session, you can begin the Writing Workshop on the first day and complete it on the second. You may need to plan for three full sessions to complete the two activities, the Writing Workshop, and the movie viewing and response questions.

ACTIVITY :: WHO'S THE WOMAN?

Part 1: Sentence Completion
- Write the Aim on the blackboard.
- Review the Lesson Vocabulary.
- Have participants form a circle.
- Refer students to the **Who's the Woman?** worksheet.
- Have participants quickly complete all the sentences in both parts (1 and 2) of the worksheet.
- Tell the participants they will read aloud their completed sentences in a specific order (e.g., Rolanda says, "A woman is strong"; Susannah says, "A woman is true").
- Go around the circle and have participants read aloud their completed statements.
- Stop the activity after all have finished reciting "A woman becomes _____."

Part 2: Brainstorm
- Tell the participants they are going to create a Who's the Woman? web.
- Reveal the prepared flip chart paper with the three labeled circles.
- Ask the participants to share their answers from Part 2 on the **Who's the Woman?** worksheet. Write their responses in the respective circles on the flip chart paper.
- If you need to expand the answers, ask questions before moving on to each category (e.g., Who's the woman in sports? Who's the woman in hip-hop? What else is expected of a woman at home? What else is forbidden to a woman in a marriage?).

Part 3: Women Switching Places
- Have participants sit in chairs in a circle.
- Important: There should be the exact number of chairs for the number of participants in the room excluding you. (No chair should be available for you.)
- Stand in the center of the circle.
- Explain that participants will be playing a variation of Switching Places, a game they played earlier.
- Remind them that in this game there will be no pushing or shoving. If anyone gets hurt, the game will end immediately.
- Instruct the seated participants that if the statement made is also true for them, they must get up from their seat and find another seat.
- Tell the class that the person in the center of the circle has to say one of the items that were brainstormed on the blackboard (e.g., "Anyone who feels their mother is 'the woman,' switch places," or "Anyone who feels a woman is expected to provide, switch places").
- The person left without a seat should stand in the center and continue the statements in the same format as written above.
- Continue until all the blackboard statements have been answered or until time runs out.

Note: Feel free to have students ask their own questions about women as well. The flip chart paper is just a springboard for further discussion.

PROCESSING QUESTIONS

1. *What was it like to define what it means to be a woman?*
2. *Did you strongly agree or disagree with any of the statements?*

3. *Did anyone else's comments surprise you?*
4. *What did you find in common and/or different?*
5. *Where do you get your ideas about what a woman is or isn't?*
6. *Why is it important to express our beliefs about what it means to be a woman?*
7. *In what ways are you comfortable expressing what being a woman means to you?*
8. *Can you stretch your comfort zone to try other ways of expressing yourself? How?*

DISCUSSION QUESTIONS

1. *Of the ideas that were expressed, which do you think are the most important?*
2. *Do any of the answers challenge your beliefs about what it means to be a woman?*
3. *Was there room for all of these ideas to coexist in the Women Switching Places game?*
4. *Can all of these ideas exist in one woman?*
5. *Do you think the expectation of being a woman has changed since your parents' time?*
6. *What does it mean to be a woman?*
7. *Are any of the expectations the same or different for men and women?*

Part 4: Sing It!
- Hand out the song lyrics you chose in advance and refer students to the **Lyric Breakdown** worksheet in the *Student Writing Companion*.
- Explain that participants will be reading a series of lyrics from well-known music artists and forming their own opinions about the subject matter.

DISCUSSION QUESTIONS

1. *Why do people choose art (e.g., music, theater) to express their beliefs?*
2. *How can you use artistic means to express your beliefs?*

CLOSING :: WHIP-AROUND

- What is one positive message that you would like to spread about women through art?

ACTIVITY TWO :: WRITING WORKSHOP: IDENTITY

- Refer participants to the questions and prompts listed in **Writing Workshop Part One: Identity** worksheet for the writing portion of this lesson.
- Give the students some time to write responses to the questions on the handouts.
- After participants complete the writing exercise, allow them to choose one of the topics that resonated with them, and tell them that they will be transforming their answer into a poem.
- Refer students to the three poem templates in their *Student Writing Companion*s: The **I Am ... Poem**, the **Hold On ... Poem**, and the **Reflection Poem**. Have them choose one of these templates.

- Have the participants use the lined worksheets for their rough drafts, and then create a finished, clean copy on the final worksheet.

 ## ACTIVITY THREE :: MOVIE VIEWING AND RESPONSE

- Show the movie *13 Going On 30* to the class or substitute a movie of your choosing on the theme of identity.
- Have the class respond to the **Movie Response Questions**.

 ## SAY MORE :: ADDITIONAL WRITING PROMPTS

If time permits, encourage participants to write more in depth by asking them to write responses to the following questions.

» What are some things that you think people say about you?

» What are some things that you wish people said about you?

» Do you have a favorite poem or quote? If so, what is it? Or, is there something that one of your friends or family members have said that sticks in your mind?

» What is it like to be a young woman at your school?

» How do you know when you become "a woman"?

Who's the Woman?

This question has always been
"Who's the man?" but now we've flipped it
and want to know, "Who's the woman?"
What are you expected to do,
what are you forbidden to do,
and what are the rules?
Today we are going to be exploring these issues
thoroughly, most definitely, definitively, through and through.

Please take a moment to complete the following statements to create a list poem. Whatever's clever, but don't take forever.

Part One: Sentence Completion

A woman is _____

A woman feels _____

A woman should _____

A woman cannot _____

A woman must _____

A woman needs _____

A woman wants _____

A woman believes _____

A woman becomes _____

Part Two: Brainstorm

Who's the woman to you?_____

A woman is expected to _____

A woman is forbidden to _____

Lyric Breakdown

1. What do the chosen lyrics have in common? Explain and give an example.

....

....

....

2. How are these lyrics different? Explain and give an example.

....

....

....

3. Choose one song and summarize its message in one sentence.

....

....

....

4. Is there a music artist today who you feel advises or addresses women and how they should be and behave? Give an example.

....

....

....

Writing Workshop Part One

Identity

1. What are three things that you want the world to know about you?

2. How do you think young women should be treated?

3. What is the best thing about being a young woman? What is the worst thing?

4. Do people have expectations of you? If so, what are they?

5. How do you think the world sees you?

6. How do you wish the world saw you?

7. What is something that you think you are good at? Something that you wish you were better at?

8. What do you think is the best part of your personality?

9. What is a part of your personality that you would like to improve?

I Am . . . Poem

Fill in the spaces below with the description in the parentheses.

I am . . .
(Sounds you heard growing up)

....

I am . . .
(Foods you eat)

....

I am . . .
(Names in your family)

....

I am . . .
(Places you lived)

....

I am . . .
(Choose a topic from the box below or create your own: _____)

....

I am . . .
(Choose a topic from the box below or create your own: _____)

....

TOPICS: music you listen to, magazines you read, hobbies you have, friends you have, family you listen to, things that make you who you are, the communities you live in, subjects you love, issues that matter to you, family traditions, nationalities, games you play, smells from your childhood

NAME

Final I Am . . . Poem

I am . . .

I am . . .

I am . . .

I am . . .

I am . . .

I am . . .

I am _____

Hold On . . . Poem

Fill in the spaces below with your thoughts on how to complete the sentence.

Hold on . . . even if . . .

Hold on . . . even if . . .

Hold on . . . even if . . .

Hold on . . . even if . . .

Hold on . . . even if . . .

Hold on . . . even if . . .

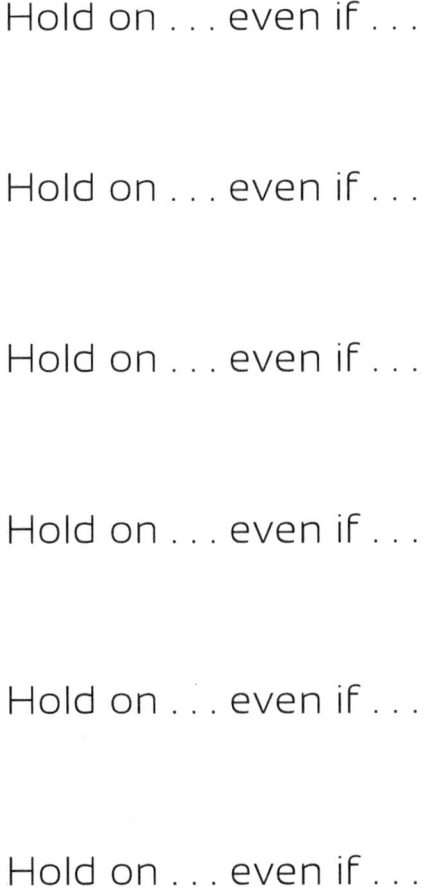

Final Hold On . . . Poem

Hold on . . . even if . . .

Hold on . . . even if . . .

Hold on . . . even if . . .

Hold on . . . even if . . .

Hold on . . . even if . . .

Hold on . . . even if . . .

Reflection Poem

Fill in the spaces below with your thoughts on how to complete the sentences.

I used to think . . .

But now I know . . .

I always thought . . .

But I never . . .

I once felt . . .

But now I see . . .

If I could . . .

I would . . .

I never . . .

But I might . . .

I can't . . .

But I can . . .

I won't . . .

But I might . . .

I used to think . . .

But now I know . . .

Final Reflection Poem

I used to think . . .

But now I know . . .

I always thought . . .

But I never . . .

I once felt . . .

But now I see . . .

If I could . . .

I would . . .

I never . . .

But I might . . .

I can't . . .

But I can . . .

I won't . . .

But I might . . .

I used to think . . .

But now I know . . .

NAME

Movie Response Questions

13 Going On 30

1. Jenna's birthday wish is to grow up. What does being grown-up mean to you?

2. There were some elements of Jenna that were completely the same as both her thirteen- and thirty-year-old self. What parts of your character do you want to retain as you get older?

3. When Jenna wakes up as a thirty-year-old she has everything she dreamed of having when she was thirteen, yet she feels like something is missing. What do you think is missing for her? What are some things that you could not be happy without?

4. There is a popular saying that goes "The grass is always greener on the other side." Why do you think people always want what they don't have?

5. Jenna learns about what she really values as she faces certain obstacles throughout the course of the movie. Have you ever had an experience that helped you better understand what you value most?

6. Why is it important to accept yourself and be at peace with who you are?

Lean on Me

OBJECTIVE
Participants will recognize the support systems available to them.

SUMMARY
Using group discussion and worksheets, participants learn which people and what resources are available when they need help.

AIM
Who can I turn to when I need support?

STANDARDS
CCSS — RI.7, W.3, W.4, SL.1, SL.2, Sl.4, L.6
SEL — Self-Awareness, Social Awareness

MATERIALS
flip chart paper, markers, *My Inner Circle*, *Who Can I Turn To?*, and *Lean on Me* worksheets, *Those You Are Closest To* writing prompts, copy of Sisterhood of the Traveling Pants DVD, and *Movie Response Questions: Sisterhood of the Traveling Pants* (pp. 47–57 in the Student Writing Companion)

Lesson Vocabulary

support v., to keep from failing or sinking; to solace; to assist; to encourage; to defend; to strengthen

PREPARE IN ADVANCE
Have a list of school resources on hand to add to the students' personal lists.

FACILITATOR NOTE
This lesson is substantial and may take a full session. If you finish the first two activities before the end of the first session, you can begin the Writing Workshop on the first day and complete it on the second. You may need to plan for three full sessions to complete the two activities, the Writing Workshop, and the movie viewing and response questions.

ACTIVITY ONE :: WHO YOU GONNA CALL?

Part 1: "Who You Gonna Call?" Brainstorm
- Read the Aim to the group, and then tell the participants that they will be talking about friendship and the different types of friends they have.
- Review Lesson Vocabulary.
- Make two columns on the flip chart paper. Label one column "Best qualities of a friend" and

the other "Worst qualities of a friend."

- Ask participants to brainstorm the best and worst qualities of a friend. Write them on the board as they are given.

DISCUSSION QUESTIONS

1. *Are there any qualities on one list that could also be on the other? Why?*
2. *Do all your friends have all the qualities on the best list?*
3. *Do you think all your friends are the same, or are they different in some ways?*
4. *Can you name the roles that some of your friends play, such as confidant or cheerleader?*

Part 2: My Inner Circle
- Pass out the **My Inner Circle** worksheet.
- Have the participants fill out the worksheet, then ask volunteers to share their responses.

DISCUSSION QUESTIONS

1. *Have you ever heard the expression "Birds of a feather"? What does it mean? Is it always true?*
2. *If you put all the people named on the worksheet in one room, do you think that they would all get along?*
3. *What did you realize about your friends when completing the worksheet?*
4. *Do you believe that it is important to have different types of friends for different situations? Why or why not?*

ACTIVITY TWO :: LEAN ON ME

Part 1: Help! I Need Somebody!
- State the Aim of the lesson.
- Review Lesson Vocabulary.

DISCUSSION QUESTIONS

1. *In general, do you believe that all people need help sometimes? What makes you think so?*

Part 2: Who Can I Turn To?
- Ask the group members to think about a time when each of the following people they know needed help, and who those people turned to:
  - A teacher
  - A parent
  - A neighbor
  - A grandparent
  - A friend
  - A teammate
- Refer students to the **Who Can I Turn To?** worksheet, and have them fill it in.
- Ask volunteers to share their responses.

 ## DISCUSSION QUESTIONS

1. *Was it easy to think of someone for all these questions?*
2. *Was there any question for which you could only think of one person? If so, why do you think that is?*

Part 3: Lean on Me
- Point participants to and have them fill out the **Lean on Me** worksheet.
- Ask volunteers to share their responses.

 ## PROCESSING QUESTIONS

1. *Was it difficult or easy to figure out whom to turn to in each situation? Why?*
2. *Did you have different answers than some of the other participants? What do those choices say about each of you?*
3. *How does it help to hear about other people's choices?*
4. *How do you feel about asking for help?*
5. *What are the benefits of getting help with a problem?*
6. *What kind of help can others count on you for?*
7. *Why do we turn to certain people when specific problems come up?*
8. *What is something you might need help with this week? Who can you turn to for help?*

 ## CLOSING :: WHIP-AROUND

- What is something you might need help with this week? Who can you turn to for help?

 ## ACTIVITY THREE :: WRITING WORKSHOP: THOSE YOU ARE CLOSEST TO

- Refer students to the **Those You Are Closest To** writing prompts in their *Student Writing Companion*s.
- Give the students some time to write responses to the questions on the handouts.

 ## ACTIVITY FOUR :: MOVIE VIEWING AND RESPONSE

- Show the movie *The Sisterhood of the Traveling Pants* to the class or substitute a movie of your choosing on the theme of Those You Are Closest To.
- Have the class respond to the **Movie Response Questions**.

 **SAY MORE** :: ADDITIONAL WRITING PROMPTS

If time permits, encourage participants to write more in depth by asking them to write responses to the following questions.

FACILITATOR NOTE

For the prompts below, be sensitive to girls in the group who may not have a mother or may not have a father in their lives. When asking these questions, adjust your language accordingly.

» What does the word "family" mean to you? Who are the key members of your family?

» What is your first memory of your family?

» Write a paragraph about the woman in your family whom you are closest with (e.g., mom, grandmother, or aunt). What is she like? How has she been a role model to you as a young woman?

» Name as many things as you can remember that you have learned from your father.

» Is there anyone in your life whom you view as a negative role model?

My Inner Circle

In the center circle, write the names of the people you consider your closest friends. In the second circle, write the names of the people you like a lot but are not the first ones who you run to with a secret. Then, in the largest circle, write the names of people you just hang out with occasionally or casually. Next to each name, write the role that the person plays in your life.

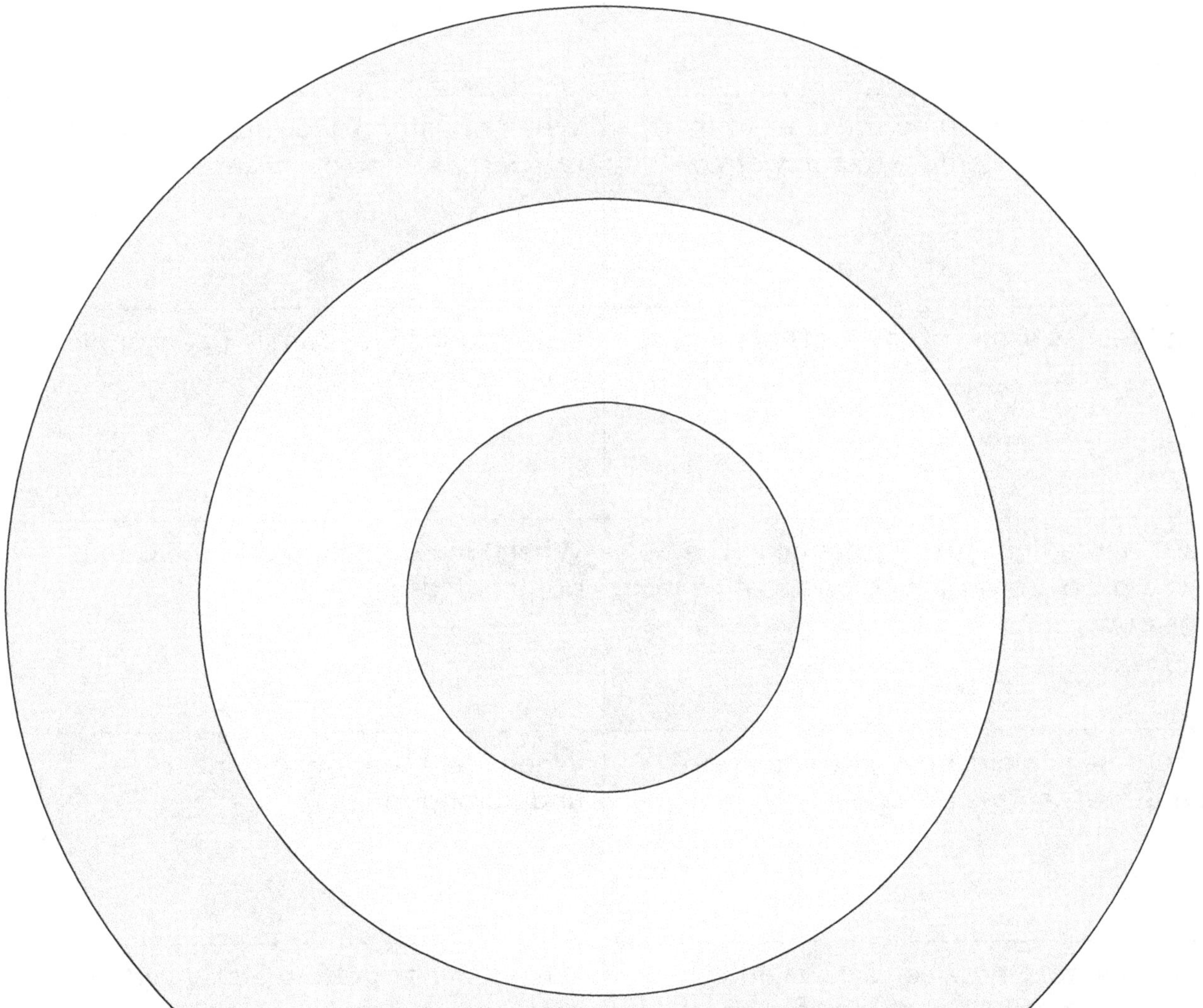

Who Can I Turn To?

In each box, write the role or name of as many people as you can think of to whom you can turn in the situation described.

When my best friend betrays me . . . (e.g., my sister Tamika, another friend)	When I need new clothes for a party and don't have any money . . .
When I don't understand the current math assignment and there's a test tomorrow . . .	When my mom/dad grounds me and there is a party tomorrow night . . .
When I feel as if one of my teachers hates me . . .	If someone in my family has a drinking or drug problem . . .
When I had a fight with someone and now I have a problem with everyone that person hangs out with . . .	When I'm not included in the group of popular kids . . .
When there is a girl/boy I like and I don't know if she/he likes me . . .	When I feel that my parents don't understand me . . .
When I feel torn between school and outside responsibilities or distractions . . .	When I'm not getting along with my brothers or sisters . . .

Lean on Me

Here are your many support systems. Fill in the names of the people in each of your planets.

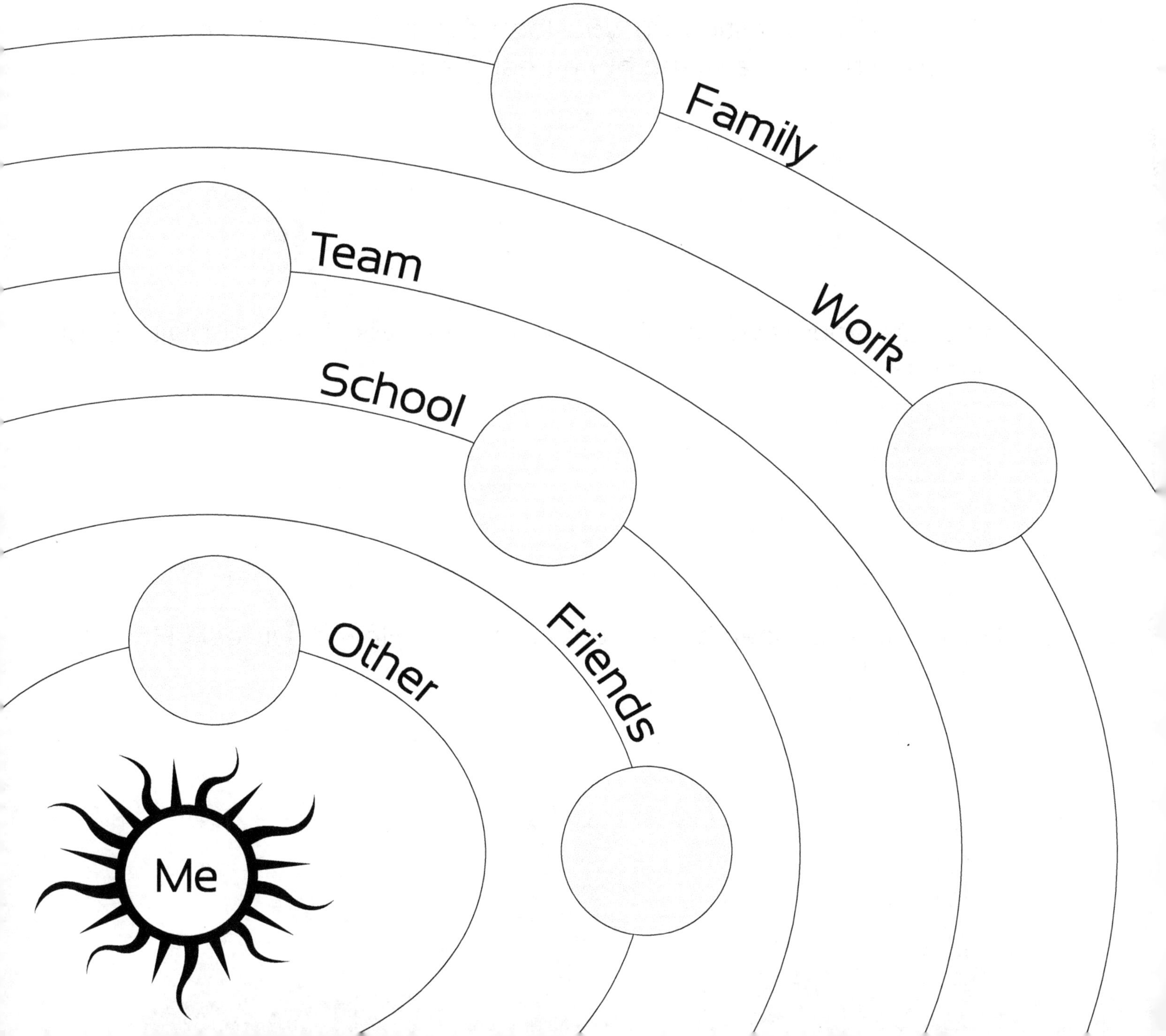

Family

Team

Work

School

Friends

Other

Me

Writing Workshop Part Two

Those You Are Closest To

Friends

1. What kind of qualities do you look for in a friend? What makes someone not just a friend but a best friend?

2. What are your favorite things to do when you hang out with your friends?

3. Have you ever been betrayed by a friend? How did it feel? How did you handle it?

4. Describe a time you were upset and a friend was there for you and helped you feel better.

5. Why do we need friends?

6. What are the most important things that your friends have taught you?

Family

1. What does it feel like to spend time around your family? What is it like being a preteen/teenage member of your family?

2. Who are the most important members of your family?

3. What is the best thing about your family?

4. What is one thing about your family that you wish could be different?

5. Why is it important to have family?

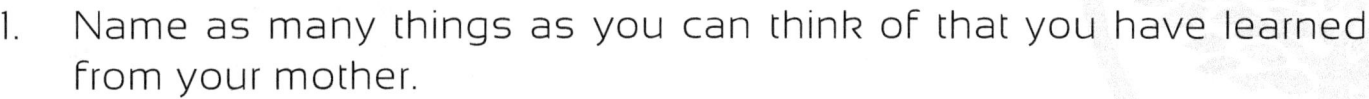

Mothers and Role Models

1. Name as many things as you can think of that you have learned from your mother.

2. In what ways are you similar to your mother? Do you look like your mother at all? In what ways?

3. In what ways are you different from your mother? Do you ever disagree with your mother? About what?

4. What kinds of dreams does your mother have for you?

5. Describe a favorite memory that you have of your mother.

6. If you could write your mother a letter thanking her for the things she has done for you, what would you say?

7. If you could write your mother a letter ten years from now telling her about the kind of woman you have become, what would you say?

8. What does it mean to be a role model? What makes someone a good role model?

9. Do you have a role model? Who? Why is this person your role model?

10. Are you a role model to anyone in your life?

11. Write shout-outs to two people who have helped you in your life.

12. Write R.I.P. shout-outs to two people whom you have loved and lost.

Movie Response Questions

The Sisterhood of the Traveling Pants

1. The four main characters have distinctly different personalities. Why do you think they are such close friends? What are the main ties that bind them?

2. Each of the girls is deeply affected by her relationship with her family. Can you think of some examples of how this is true? How has your relationship with your family shaped you?

3. Each of the girls must face a huge obstacle by the time the summer is over. How does facing these obstacles shape their character?

4. What do you think is the greatest gift that these girls give to one another through their friendship? What gifts do you give to those you love through your relationship with them?

5. In many ways these girls are one another's extended family. Do you have people you consider to be members of your family whom you are not related to by blood? What are the criteria to include someone in your "created family"?

6. How do you define the term "sisterhood?" How does this term apply to your experience in HERstory?

Body Positive!

OBJECTIVE
Participants will understand the importance of appreciating their body.

SUMMARY
Participants recognize and appreciate the internal and external components of the body.

AIM
How can I appreciate my body?

STANDARDS
*CCSS – RI.1, RI.7, W.3, W.4, W.7, SL.1, SL.2, SL.4, L.6
SEL – Self-Awareness, Social Awareness*

MATERIALS
*Get Plump ad handout, **Body Intelligence** and **Body Appreciation** worksheets, **Body Image** writing prompts, Real Women Have Curves DVD, and **Movie Response Questions: Real Women Have Curves** (pp. 58–66 in the Student Writing Companion)*

Lesson Vocabulary

appreciate v., to understand the worth or importance of (something or someone); to be grateful for

body image n., a subjective picture of one's own physical appearance established both by self-observation and by noting the reactions of others

plump adj., having a full, rounded, usually pleasing form

standard n., something that is considered to be a model for measurement or comparison, or serves as an accepted authority

stereotype n., a usually oversimplified and inaccurate idea held in common by many people

subjective adj., affected or shaped by personal experiences, beliefs, and feelings

FACILITATOR NOTE

This lesson is substantial and may take a full session. If you finish the first two activities before the end of the first session, you can begin the Writing Workshop on the first day and complete it on the second. You may need to plan for three full sessions to complete the two activities, the Writing Workshop, and the movie viewing and response questions.

Tell participants that these worksheets will not be collected. Due to the sensitivity of this lesson, it is important that participants know this so that they will be more willing to answer the questions honestly.

ACTIVITY ONE :: BODY INTELLIGENCE

Part 1: Owning It!
- State the Aim on a sheet of flip chart paper.
- Review Lesson Vocabulary.
- Refer students to the **Get Plump** ad.
- Have volunteers read sections of the ad aloud.
- Ask participants to note the date of the ad.
- Ask how they feel about the ad and if they think standards of beauty have changed.

DISCUSSION QUESTIONS

1. *Can you think of anyone who strikes you as beautiful but defies certain conventional standards of beauty? What conventional standard is she breaking?*
2. *What makes this person attractive to you? Do you think she is ashamed of her body? Why or why not?*
3. *Can you think of anyone who has overcome a physical setback to achieve his or her dream (e.g., a one-armed pitcher on a baseball team)?*
4. *What kind of attitude do you think that person embodied to overcome the challenge?*
5. *What stereotypes can you think of that deal with body images based on particular cultures or ethnicities? Where do these stereotypes come from? Are they true or false?*
6. *Do you feel anyone has the perfect body?*

Part 2: Body Intelligence
- Refer students to the **Body Intelligence** worksheet.
- Give participants eight to ten minutes to complete the worksheet.
- Ask for volunteers to share their answers with the class.
- Continue to use the worksheet as a foundation to initiate the discussion.

DISCUSSION QUESTIONS

1. *How does it feel to reflect on and talk about your body?*
2. *Do you think our bodies are a sensitive topic to discuss? Why or why not?*
3. *Did the exercise bring to your attention anything about your body that surprised you?*
4. *What types of habits can you establish that will make you more conscious of your body—not necessarily more attractive, but more aware of what your body needs?*
5. *Some people regard their body as their temple. What are some ways to praise your body unconditionally as a temple?*
6. *What does your body mean to you?*

Part 3: Body Appreciation
- Have students fill out the **Body Appreciation** worksheet.

PROCESSING QUESTIONS

1. *How did it feel to identify what your body has done for you?*
2. *Is it challenging to appreciate your body?*
3. *Is it important to feel comfortable in your own skin?*
4. *What was it like to hear other girls talk about their body challenges and appreciation?*
5. *What conclusions can you draw from these observations?*
6. *How can you take the best care of the body you have at your age?*

CLOSING :: WHIP-AROUND

- Read from the **Body Appreciation** worksheet the item that you feel is the most important thing your body has done for you lately.

ACTIVITY TWO :: WRITING WORKSHOP: BODY IMAGE

- Make copies of the appropriate **Body Image** writing prompts at the end of this lesson.
- Give the students some time to write responses to the questions on the handouts.

ACTIVITY THREE :: MOVIE VIEWING AND RESPONSE

- Show the movie *Real Women Have Curves* to the class or substitute a movie of your choosing on the theme of Body Image.
- Have the class respond to the **Movie Response Questions.**

SAY MORE :: ADDITIONAL WRITING PROMPTS

If time permits, encourage participants to write more in depth by asking them to write responses to the following questions.

» Do you have any favorite quotes or poems on the subject of body image?

» How does your family think you should dress?

» How do your friends think you should dress?

» Who do you think sets the standard of how young women should look?

RITTER & CO.

Fremont Street at Second

Available After Jan. 3, 1891

DEALERS IN FINE GENERAL MERCHANDISE

RESPECTFULLY TELL THE LADIES

GET PLUMP

WITH PROFESSOR WILLIAMS' FAMED

"FAT-TEN-U" FOODS

Before

After

Why suffer tortures with inferior mechanical devices that artificially fatten? Don't look like the poor unfortunate on the left who, shorn of her artificial inflationary devices & pads, must, in the confines of her bedroom, through shame, try to cover her poor thin figure from the gaze of her beloved spouse.

A Testimonial

The accompanying portrait is that of Sarah MacHenry, Philadelphia, posing with her two sisters, who writes:

"In four weeks Professor William's famed FAT-TEN-U FOODS increased my weight 39 pounds, gave me new womanly vigor & developed me finely. My two sisters also use FAT-TEN-U and have gained much needed fleshiness. Because of our newly found vigor we have taken up Grecian Dancing and have leading roles in all local productions."

And Despair

These foods cure nerve and brain exhaustion, which you know as general debility. They make pale folks pink and thin folks plump and weak folks well and despairing folks happy. They will make you young all your life. You know it is better to be a young old woman than an old young woman!

No tonics, nervines, sarsaparilline, or other medicines are necessary when FAT-TEN-U FOODS are taken. $1.00 a bottle at RITTER AND CO.

Professor William's "Fat-Ten-U" Foods are guaranteed to make The Thin

Plump & Rosy with HONEST Fleshiness of Form

Body Intelligence

Take a few minutes to answer the following questions.

WHICH PART OR ASPECT OF MY BODY . . .

- is the strongest? _____
- is the weakest? _____
- is the most injury-prone? _____
- am I most comfortable with? _____
- am I least comfortable with? _____
- do other people notice first? _____
- do I really like but other people notice least? _____
- do I appreciate the most? _____

"IF YOU LIVED IN YOUR BODY, YOU'D BE HOME NOW."

Pretend you could move out of your body and someone new could move in. What tips would you give the new tenant about what it's like to live here? Consider the following:

What kind of care does this body need?

- Rest _____
- Feeding _____
- Watering _____
- Sunlight/Outdoors _____
- Physical Activity/Play _____
- Mental Stimulation _____
- Soothing/Peace _____
- Healing _____

- How do other people respond to this body?

- What tips can you pass on about how to manage this body?

- How does this body learn a new physical or mental skill? (Do you learn visually, audibly, through movement, etcetera?)

- Our bodies hear everything we think or say about ourselves. Take a moment to write a letter to your body. Tell it what you appreciate about it.

Dear _____,

Thank you for taking the time to listen to what I have to say. I appreciate you as much as you appreciate me!

With Love, _____

Body Appreciation

What has your body done for you lately?

- Fought off an infection
- Let you hear your favorite music
- Stayed awake so you could study for an exam
- Learned a new skill
- Rewarded you with the sight of a sunset
- Healed a bruise
- Let you enjoy a delicious meal
- Gotten stronger
- Enjoyed the wonderful smell of fresh flowers
- Kept working despite being in pain
- Expressed a strong emotion through your face and body language
- Defended you from an attack or healed from an attack
- Let you know through pain that something needed your attention
- Released you from pain
- Took a walk through the park
- Hugged someone you love
- Rejuvenated during sleep
- Danced all night long

Set aside some time each day to thank and appreciate the many capacities of your body.

Writing Workshop Part Three

Body Image

1. Do you think that young women in general have a positive body image? Why or why not?

2. Do you feel that you have a positive body image? Why or why not?

3. What messages do you think TV, movies, and magazines give young women about what their bodies should look like? About the way they dress?

4. What messages do you receive from your family about how you should look? From your friends?

5. What messages are young women given about going through puberty? How does going through puberty feel?

6. How do you feel about your body? Do you feel any pressure about having to look a certain way? Are you comfortable in your body? Why or why not?

7. Have you ever received a compliment related to how you look? An insult related to how you look? How did each one feel?

8. Have you ever insulted another girl about how she looks? Why do you
    think girls insult one another about their appearances?

9. List some compliments that women hear about their bodies and some
    insults that women hear about their bodies.

10. In the form of your own poem, what would you like to say to the world
    about the issue of young women's body image?

Movie Response Questions

Real Women Have Curves

1. In the movie, Anna receives a lot of different messages about her body. In general, there are a lot of messages aimed at women about their bodies. How do we know which ones to listen to?

2. What kind of culture did Anna grow up in? How do the expectations placed upon her affect the way people perceive her body? How does it affect the way she perceives her body?

3. Anna's parents do not believe that she should go to college but that instead she should work in the factory. What do you believe is right for Anna? How do we know what is right for us as individuals?

4. Have you ever wanted to show that you could exceed people's expectations? Explain.

5. Anna's actions in the garment factory inspire the women she works with to reveal the true nature of and celebrate their bodies. Why is it important for women to love and honor their bodies?

6. Anna stands up for how she believes women should be treated. What power do you have to set the tone for and create new traditions and expectations for the next generation of women?

Make a Connection

OBJECTIVE

Participants will understand what positive qualities they have to offer and will identify the qualities that they think are important in a mate.

SUMMARY

Participants will play a game and write their own personal singles ads to delineate their positive qualities in a relationship, and they will prioritize the qualities that are important in a mate.

AIM

What positive qualities do I have to offer?

STANDARDS

*CCSS – RI.7, W.3, W.4, SL.1, SL.2, SL.4, L.6
SEL – Self-Awareness, Social Awareness, Relationship Skills, Responsible Decision Making*

MATERIALS

*one wide-mouth empty bottle, **Spin the Bottle** sheet, scissors, **Create Your Own Personals Ad** and **Rate Your Mate** worksheets, **Love and Relationships** writing prompts, copy of Enchanted DVD, **Movie Response Questions: Enchanted** (pp. 67–73 in the Student Writing Companion)*

Lesson Vocabulary

appeal n., the quality that makes somebody or something pleasant or desirable

ideal n., perfect example

love n., an intense feeling of tender affection, compassion, passionate attraction, and/or desire

mate n., member of a relationship

qualities n., distinguishing characteristics

relationship n., an emotional or other connection between persons, an involvement

FACILITATOR NOTE

This lesson is substantial and may take a full session. If you finish the first two activities before the end of the first session, you can begin the Writing Workshop on the first day and complete it on the second. You may need to plan for three full sessions to complete the two activities, the Writing Workshop, and the movie viewing and response questions.

PREPARE IN ADVANCE

Make two copies of the Spin the Bottle sheet from the end of this lesson and cut them into twenty separate pieces.

ACTIVITY ONE :: MAKE A CONNECTION

Part 1: Spin the Bottle

- Write the Aim on the board.
- Review Lesson Vocabulary.
- Tell participants they are going to be playing a variation of the game Spin the Bottle.

- Have the participants sit in a circle.
- Lay the plastic bottle in the middle of the circle.
- Appoint one participant to spin the bottle.
- After the bottle stops spinning, have the person the bottle points to pick a slip of paper from the bottle and read aloud the instruction.
- Have the participant do what the paper instructs.
- When the participant is finished, have her set the paper aside and spin the bottle again to determine who will have the next turn.
- Repeat the instruction and spin the bottle for three to five rounds or until all the papers have been read, if time allows.

Part 2: Create Your Own Personals Ad
- Refer students to the **Create Your Own Personals Ad** worksheet.
- Instruct participants that they have about fifteen minutes to complete the worksheet. Explain that this is a silent, individual activity, as they are reflecting only on themselves.

DISCUSSION QUESTIONS

1. *What was it like to create your own personals ad?*
2. *Does your headline fit your overall profile?*
3. *How do you know what your positive qualities are?*
4. *What do you feel is the greatest quality you have to offer?*
5. *Why is it important to consider your positive goals?*
6. *Did you focus on any particular part of your personality or think of any particular attributes? Your intelligence? Your talents? Your physical ability?*
7. *What are some of the important qualities that anyone would need in a relationship?*
8. *Do you look for the same positive attributes in yourself as in other people?*

Part 3: Rate Your Mate
- Brainstorm with the group the personality traits of the ideal mate.

FACILITATOR NOTE
Steer the brainstorm toward personality traits and qualities rather than physical attributes.

- Pass out the **Rate Your Mate** worksheet.
- Read the directions aloud and tell students they have five minutes to complete the worksheet.
- Ask a few students to share what they ranked as the number 1 quality, then ask for their number 15, and then their number 7.
- Have the class vote by a show of hands on all the qualities most important to them.

PROCESSING QUESTIONS

1. *How did it feel to rate your mate?*
2. *What were the top five qualities agreed on by the majority? Why do you think that is?*
3. *What were the bottom five qualities agreed on by the majority? Why do you think that is?*
4. *If you added a quality, what was it and explain why?*

5. *Why is it important to think about the qualities you're looking for in a mate?*
6. *How can what you discovered today help you navigate relationships?*

DISCUSSION QUESTIONS

1. *How realistic do you feel this is? Do you actually consider these qualities when you become or think about becoming romantically involved with someone?*
2. *Is it better to imagine your future love or be surprised?*

CLOSING :: WHIP-AROUND

- What personal quality are you currently most proud of?

ACTIVITY TWO :: WRITING WORKSHOP: LOVE AND RELATIONSHIPS

- Make copies of the appropriate **Love and Relationships** writing prompts at the end of this lesson.
- Give the students some time to write responses to the questions on the handouts.

ACTIVITY THREE :: MOVIE VIEWING AND RESPONSE

- Show the movie *Enchanted* to the class or substitute a movie of your choosing on the theme of love and relationships.
- Have the class respond to the **Movie Response Questions**.

SAY MORE :: ADDITIONAL WRITING PROMPTS

If time permits, encourage participants to write more in depth by asking them to write responses to the following questions.

» Why do you think people get into romantic relationships? Do you like being in a relationship?

» What is the best thing about being in a relationship?

» What is the worst thing about being in a relationship?

» Why do you think people stay in relationships that are unhealthy?

» When it comes to issues of relationships and sex, do you think that men and women are judged differently?

» Why do you think teen pregnancy occurs so frequently? Do you have any friends who are teen parents? What is that experience like for them?

» Do you think teenagers receive enough education about how to protect their sexual health? What do you think is the most important information for teenagers to know regarding their sexual health?

Spin the Bottle

Say one thing you like about yourself.	What power do you think you would have if you were a superhero?
Brag about one impressive thing you've done.	Say one positive thing you think you have to offer.
Tell one wish you have for yourself.	I am a good friend because . . .
I feel I am unique because . . .	Express one talent you have.
Say one positive word that begins with the first letter of your first name.	Say one positive thing you imagine for your future.

Create Your Own Personals Ad

Create your own personals ad. Describe yourself. Be creative and specific. Don't lie! Spark the interest of your ideal match! Tell what your friends say are your award-winning qualities. Round out your profile with interesting information that highlights your unique personality, background, and interests. Go beyond the ordinary and offer up details. Keep in mind the compliments that were made about you during the Spin the Bottle game.

I am a _____, and I am _____ years old. I live in _____ _____.

I can describe my personality as _____.

I feel I am unique because _____

For fun I like to _____ _____.

My favorite way to spend my time is _____.

I am not interested in _____.

Some of the goals I want to achieve are _____, _____,

and _____.

When I think of the places I want to visit, _____ comes to mind.

Love means _____ _____ _____.

When I think of friendship, I think of _____ _____

To be totally honest, I want _____ _____

I often dream of _____.

I feel life is _____.

My friends often describe me as _____ _____

Some of the things I have to offer in a relationship are _____ _____ _____

Rate Your Mate

Have you ever imagined the person you might want to share your life with? Think of your *ideal* mate. Number the qualities below from 1 to 17: Number 1 means the quality is most important and number 17 means this quality is unimportant. Remember to use a different number for each!

_____ You share the same interests and enjoy doing things together.

_____ You get along with each other's families.

_____ You have the same friends.

_____ You find her/him physically attractive.

_____ He/She has money.

_____ You have similar personalities.

_____ You feel a passionate love for each other.

_____ You have similar goals and hopes for the future.

_____ He/She is a good communicator.

_____ Your desires about children and raising a family are the same.

_____ You share the same values and ethics.

_____ You both enjoy the same foods.

_____ He/She makes you laugh.

_____ You are friends first.

_____ You share the same religious beliefs.

_____ You are of the same race and cultural background.

_____ Fill in your own quality _____

Writing Workshop Part Four

Love and Relationships

Questions for Everyone

1. What does it feel like to have a crush?

2. Have you ever been in love? How does it feel?

3. Have you ever had your heart broken or gone through a breakup? How does/did it feel?

4. What makes someone attractive to you?

5. If you have an ex, is there anything you would still like to say to that person? Write it down.

6. Have you ever had a conflict with one of your friends over someone you were both interested in? What was that like?

7. How would you describe a first kiss?

8. How are young women treated in relationships? How should they be treated? How do you want to be treated in a relationship?

9. Write a love poem in any form that you wish. Allow your words to flow freely.

10. Is it easy or hard to trust someone in a relationship? Why?

11. Are there certain perceptions about how men should conduct themselves in a relationship? Are the perceptions about how women should conduct themselves different from those for men?

Movie Response Questions

Enchanted

1. Giselle's world morphed from one distinct reality to another. Do you ever feel like your reality is constantly changing?

2. Giselle was a very trusting character who was dedicated to her quest for love. What does trust have to do with love?

3. In the film, the expression of love is depicted in many different forms. If you had to demonstrate love as actions without words, what would those actions be?

4. In the film, Robert and Nancy learned that the best way to love each other was to let each other go. How do we know when to hold on and when to let go?

5. The plot of this movie offers a modern twist on the typical fairy-tale structure. For example, Giselle rescues Robert in the end instead of the typical "knight rescuing the maiden" scenario. How do you think women's roles in relationships have changed since your parents' time? What do you think the most important role of a woman in a relationship should be?

6. If you could write a modern fairy-tale ending to your own love story, what would it be?

Great Expectations!

OBJECTIVE

Participants will identify their visions and dreams.

SUMMARY

Through brainstorming, writing, and dialogue, participants identify and share the future they envision for themselves.

AIM

How do I envision myself in the future?

STANDARDS

CCSS – RI.7, W.3, W.4, SL.1, SL.2, SL.4, L.6
SEL – Self-Awareness

MATERIALS

CD player/MP3 player and speakers, flip chart paper, markers, **For Just One Day** *and* **Great Expectations!** *worksheets,* **Dreams** *writing prompts, copy of* Take the Lead *DVD, and* **Movie Response Questions: Take the Lead** *(pp. 74–79 in the Student Writing Companion)*

Lesson Vocabulary

calling n., a strong urge to follow a particular career or do a particular type of work

envision v., to form a mental picture of something, typically something that may occur or be possible in the future

expectations n., things looked forward to; a prospect of future good

imagination n., the ability to form images and ideas in the mind, especially of things never seen or never experienced directly

FACILITATOR NOTE

Choose either Warm-Up according to the strengths of the group. This lesson is substantial and may take a full session. If you finish Activity One before the end of the first session, you can begin the Writing Workshop on the first day and complete it on the second. You may need to plan for three full sessions to complete Activity One, the Writing Workshop, and the movie viewing and response questions.

 ## WARM-UP ONE :: FOR JUST ONE DAY: MOVEMENT VERSION

- Inform participants they are going to imagine being different people for just one day.
- Explain that they should walk around quickly when the music plays and stop when the music stops.
- Start the music and let it play for a few moments.
- Stop the music.
- Have participants find a partner.
- Ask participants to choose one person from history whom they would like to be for one day.
- Instruct the pairs of participants to tell each other whom they chose and why. Tell them that each participant has one minute to talk.
- Repeat the process with the following two categories:

- A celebrity
- A fictional character

WARM-UP TWO :: FOR JUST ONE DAY: WRITING VERSION

- Inform participants they are going to imagine being different people for just one day.
- Refer students to the **For Just One Day** worksheet.
- Instruct the participants to fill in the blanks, naming one person in each of the categories whom they would like to be for just one day and why:
  - A person from history
  - A celebrity
  - A fictional character
- Ask volunteers to share their choices with the class.

DISCUSSION QUESTIONS

1. *How easy or hard was it to think of someone? Why do you think that was?*
2. *What might be the benefit of identifying who you admire?*
3. *Did you see any patterns in the figures that you chose? In the figures who were chosen by the rest of the group?*

ACTIVITY ONE :: GREAT EXPECTATIONS!

Part 1: Calling Brainstorm
- Ask participants to name different careers, callings, occupations, and fields of work they have heard about or are interested in.
- If participants need prompting you may ask questions such as:
  - What are you really good at doing?
  - What do you love to do?
  - If you could spend one day working with a person in any career or calling, what would that career or calling be?
  - What other fields of work have you heard about or seen in the movies and on television that you would like to know more about?
  - What other occupations do people participate in?
- Record the answers on flip chart paper.

Part 2: Great Expectations!
- Refer students to the **Great Expectations!** worksheet.
- Review examples with the group to clarify the distinction between dreams and visions for the purposes of this activity.
- Ask participants to fill in some of their dreams and visions.

PROCESSING QUESTIONS

1. *How did it feel to talk about your dreams and visions?*
2. *Did you notice if anyone shared similar dreams?*
3. *Did you notice any dreams and visions that you had never thought of?*
4. *In general, why is it important for a person to know their dreams?*
5. *How does knowing what your specific dreams are affect your life?*

CLOSING :: WHIP-AROUND

• What is one step on the road to your dreams that you can take now?

ACTIVITY TWO :: WRITING WORKSHOP: DREAMS

• Make copies of the appropriate **Dreams** writing prompts at the end of this lesson.
• Give the students some time to write responses to the questions on the handouts.

ACTIVITY THREE :: MOVIE VIEWING AND RESPONSE

• Show the movie *Take the Lead* to the class or substitute a movie of your choosing on the theme of dreams.
• Have the class respond to the **Movie Response Questions**.

SAY MORE :: ADDITIONAL WRITING PROMPTS

If time permits, encourage participants to write more in depth by asking them to write responses to the following questions.

» Do you have any dreams that family or friends discourage? What are those dreams? Why do you think people discourage you from pursuing them?

» Have your dreams changed in the past five years? What is different about them now than five years ago?

» Why is it important to have dreams for the future?

» What would you like to say to those who encourage your dreams? To those who discourage your dreams?

For Just One Day

I would like to be _____
for just one day because . . .   (name of person from history)

I would like to be _____
for just one day because . . .   (name of celebrity)

I would like to be _____
for just one day because . . .   (name of fictional character)

Great Expectations!

I dream of . . .	What I envision happening and how I feel . . .	And it looks like . . .
Example: Going to college	Getting accepted at a college of my choice. I feel proud, smart, and competent. I can do this!	A letter in the mail, and then a beautiful campus where I am walking with new friends whom I met on my way to a class I really like.
Example: Being a star athlete	I win an Olympic gold medal and I feel like I'm on top of the world! Strong and successful.	Me on the podium with the medal around my neck and my fist raised, hearing the national anthem being played.

Choose one of the dreams above. How were you able to identify this as one of your dreams? (Example: I think about it all the time.)

In column one, put a star next to the dream(s) that come from your heart and a check next to the dream(s) that were influenced by other people in your life.

Writing Workshop Part Five

Dreams

1. What kind of dreams do you have for your future? What do you think you would like to be when you grow up?

2. Imagine yourself at age twenty-five. Where are you? What are you doing? Who are you with?

3. Do you think your dreams will come true? Why or why not?

4. What do you need to accomplish your dreams?

5. Who inspires you to keep chasing your dreams?

6. What kind of life do you dream about having?

7. What dreams does your family have for you?

8. Write a poem about what it feels like to have and chase a dream.

Movie Response Questions

Take the Lead

1. In this movie, the students have to take a leap of faith to trust Mr. Dulaine and follow his methods. When was a time that you had to take a leap of faith? What were the results?

2. In the movie, several characters face choices that will affect the course of their lives. Have you ever made a choice to follow one dream over another? Explain.

3. How can learning about someone's dreams help you better understand that person?

4. Have you ever been in a situation where your dreams were in direct conflict with someone else's? How can you resolve this type of situation?

5. Mr. Dulaine helped his students and in the process appeared to help himself. How can helping other people achieve their dreams affect your own dreams?

6. In one of the movie scenes, Rock notices LaRhette smiling to herself with her eyes closed as she dances, and when he asks her why, she responds, "Because it's my moment." What does your moment look like? What does it feel like?

Around My Way

OBJECTIVE

Participants will identify how their communities influence their lives.

SUMMARY

Participants fill out a worksheet and then discuss how their environments, communities, and heritage or traditions shape their lives.

AIM

How has my environment shaped my life?

STANDARDS

CCSS – RI.7, W.3, W.4, SL.1, SL.2, SL.4, L.6
SEL – Self-Awareness, Social Awareness

MATERIALS

Around My Way and Show Your Pride worksheets, Heritage or Tradition writing prompts, I Am from . . . Poem worksheet, copy of The Great Debaters DVD, and Movie Response Questions: The Great Debaters (pp. 80–89 in the Student Writing Companion)

Lesson Vocabulary

environment n., the sum of social and cultural conditions that influence the life of an individual or community

influence v., to have an effect on the condition or development of

slogan n., a motto; a short phrase used to summarize a principle or political message, or to advertise a product

symbol n., an action or object that expresses or represents a particular idea or quality

FACILITATOR NOTE

This lesson is substantial and may take a full session. If you finish Activity One before the end of the first session, you can begin the Writing Workshop on the first day and complete it on the second. You may need to plan for three full sessions to complete Activity One, the Writing Workshop, and the movie viewing and response questions.

ACTIVITY ONE :: AROUND MY WAY

Part 1: Around My Way Chant

- Read the Aim and then tell participants that they will be discussing how their environment has influenced their lives.
- Review Lesson Vocabulary.
- Explain to participants that they are going to make up a cheer/chant about where they are from. Tell them to be as creative as possible, and that they may include choreography.
- Divide the participants into groups of four to five depending on class size.
- In their groups, have participants decide on a common theme for their cheer. Offer suggestions, such as neighborhood, country of origin, state, city, borough, or country in which they live now.

- Give participants five minutes to come up with a cheer.
- Have each group present their cheer/chant.

DISCUSSION QUESTIONS

1. *Was it hard to decide on a common theme in your group? Why?*
2. *Were you able to come up with positive things to say about the place you chose to represent?*
3. *Were you proud of the place that you decided to represent? Why or why not?*

Part 2: Around My Way Worksheet
- Pass out the **Around My Way** worksheet.
- Have participants fill out the worksheet.
- Ask for two or three volunteers to share what they wrote.

PROCESSING QUESTIONS

1. *Was it easy or hard to think of ways that where you are from affects you? Why or why not?*
2. *Do you think that the effect your community has had on you has been positive or negative?*
3. *What effect does this community have on you? In what ways do you have an effect on this community?*
4. *What are some ways we see evidence that people impact their communities?*
5. *What is one thing you can do to have a positive impact on your community?*

DISCUSSION QUESTIONS

1. *What is negative about your environment that you can't control? How does that make you feel?*
2. *What is negative about your environment that you can control?*
3. *Do you think that you would be the same person if you grew up somewhere else? Why or why not?*

Part 3: T-Shirt Slogan Worksheet
- Have participants fill in the **Show Your Pride** T-shirt slogan worksheet.
- Explain that not only can they use words but also symbols.
- Ask participants to share their T-shirts and tell the group about the words and images that they chose.

DISCUSSION QUESTIONS

1. *Was it easy or challenging to create the T-shirt slogan?*
2. *Is it important to consider your feelings about your heritage or tradition?*
3. *Why is it important to identify what you are proud of about yourself and where you are from?*

CLOSING :: WHIP AROUND

- Have each participant share why they chose their T-shirt slogan.

ACTIVITY TWO :: WRITING WORKSHOP: HERITAGE OR TRADITION

- Make copies of the appropriate **Heritage or Tradition** writing prompts at the end of this lesson.
- Give the students some time to write responses to the questions on the handouts.
- After participants complete their answers to these questions, give them an opportunity to create an **I Am from . . . Poem** on the associated worksheet.

ACTIVITY THREE :: MOVIE VIEWING AND RESPONSE

- Show the movie *The Great Debaters* to the class or substitute a movie of your choosing on the theme of heritage or tradition.
- Have the class respond to the **Movie Response Questions**.

SAY MORE :: ADDITIONAL WRITING PROMPTS

If time permits, encourage participants to write more in depth by asking them to write responses to the following questions.

» Describe your favorite thing about the art, music, or literature of your ancestors.

» What do you wish you knew more about when you think of your ancestors or heritage?

» What traditions from your family or heritage would you like to pass on if you have children?

Around My Way

Take a moment to think about where you are from, where you live, and even the block you live on, and how all these places influence the person you are. Now answer the following questions.

1. How has living in this country influenced who you are?

2. If your family is from another country or if you have ever lived in another country, how has that influenced who you are?

3. What town do you live in?

4. How has this town influenced who you are?

5. What neighborhood do you live in?

6. How has this neighborhood influenced who you are?

7. What block do you live on?

8. How has your block influenced who you are?

9. Which one of these influences you the most? Why?

10. Which one of these influences you the least? Why?

Show Your Pride

Create a slogan for a T-shirt that represents your heritage or tradition.

Example: "New York: What Dreams Are Made Of"

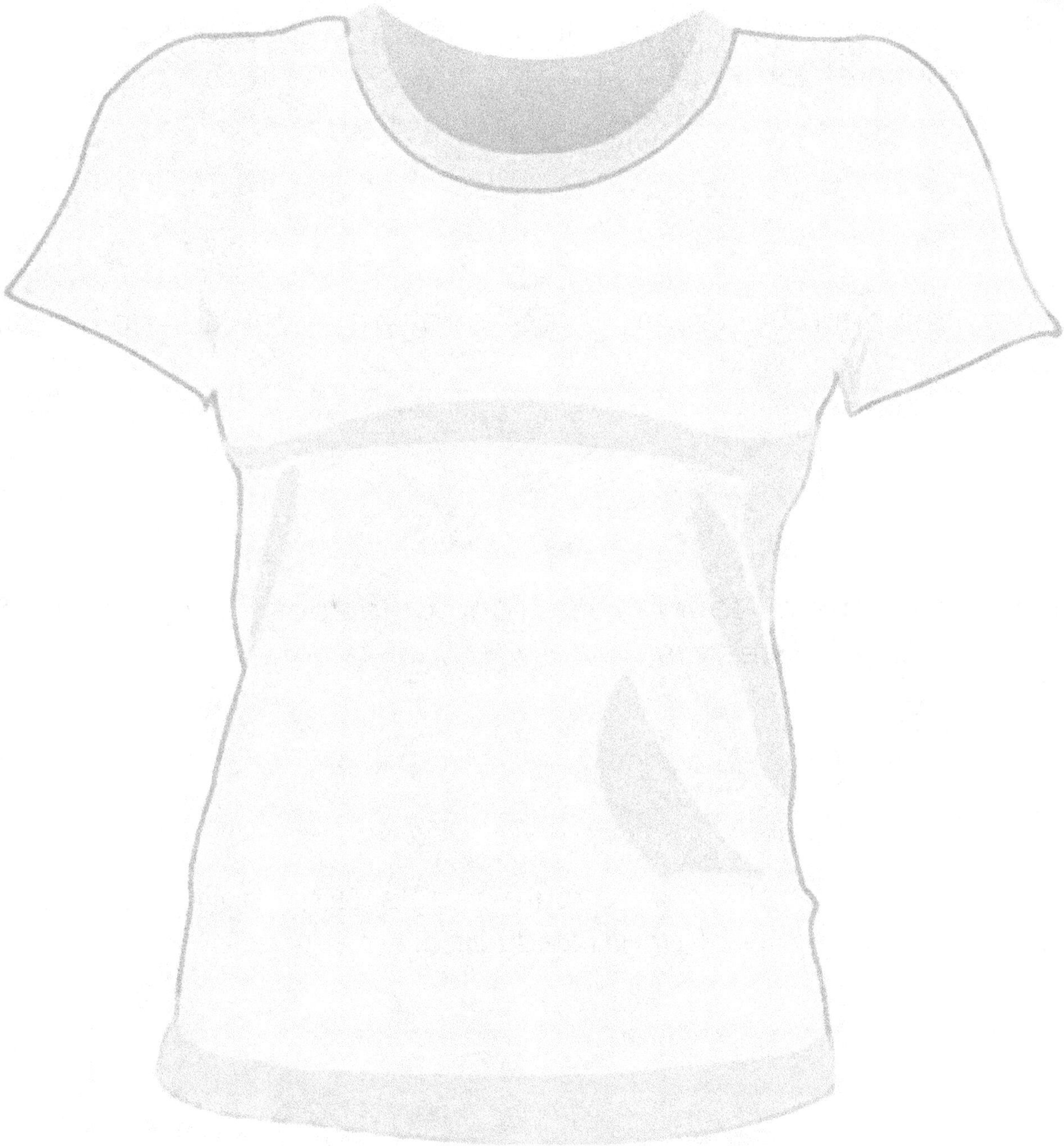

Writing Workshop Part Six

Heritage or Tradition

1. What are you most proud of about your heritage or tradition? What are you most proud of about where you and your family or your ancestors are from?

2. Describe your favorite part of the country that you consider yourself to be from.

3. Describe some of your favorite food or recipes handed down from your family or ancestors.

4. Describe some of your favorite rituals (e.g., holidays) that your ancestors or family of origin traditionally celebrate.

5. How are women treated in your family or cultural heritage? What is a woman's role? How do you feel about that?

6. If you or your family are not from the local area, are there any differences between the way women act where you are from and the way women act where you live now?

7. Does your heritage affect who you are? How?

8. What would you like to teach people about your heritage or your family?

I Am from . . . Poem

Answer the following prompts thoroughly:

- Where were you born?

- What is your family's heritage or tradition?

- Name two members of your family, living or deceased, whom you admire and why.

- Describe a family tradition.

- Describe two family customs.

- Describe a favorite family story.

- What is the first street address you remember from your childhood?

- Describe a household item, and name two household item brands.

- Describe a favorite part of your home using three sensory details.

- Name some favorite toys from your childhood.

- Name some favorite articles of clothing from your childhood.

- Name some favorite foods someone in your family made on special occasions, as well as who made them.

- Name some favorite games you played as a child.

- Name a secret place you liked to go to as a child.

- What is something an adult has said to you to encourage or praise you?

- What are some titles or lyrics from your favorite songs as a teenager?

- Name some heroes from history or literature.

- What is a dream you have for yourself?

Final I Am from . . . Poem

I am from_____. From _____ and

from _____. I am from _____.

I am from _____, from _____,

and _____. I am from _____. I

am from _____. From _____ and

from _____. Etcetera.

Movie Response Questions

The Great Debaters

1. The debate team students were from the same community and yet had very different perspectives about where they were from. How does the way we are raised affect how we view our heritage or tradition?

2. What does the term "heritage" mean to you? What does "tradition" mean? How about "blood," "ethnicity," "family," and "community"?

3. Are the students of Wiley College proud of their heritage? What does it mean to be proud of your heritage or tradition?

4. Have you ever been in a situation where you were judged as different because of your heritage or traditions? How did you react?

5. What is the best way to educate people about your heritage or tradition?

6. Samantha Booke is a groundbreaking character because she is the first female member of the debate team. Do you think young women today can consider trailblazing women such as Samantha part of their heritage? How have the women before us set the stage for us to succeed today?

The Road Less Traveled

OBJECTIVE
Participants will identify the legacy that they hope to create for themselves.

SUMMARY
Through written, verbal, and artistic means, participants will articulate their hopes for their own legacy.

AIM
Why is it important to understand the legacy that we would like to leave?

STANDARDS
CCSS – RL.1, RL.6, RI.7, W.3, W.4, SL.1, SL.2, SL.4, L.6
SEL – Self-Awareness, Social Awareness

MATERIALS
*the **Imagine** worksheet, **"The Road Not Taken"** handout, and the **Map of Your Dreams** worksheet, **Legacy** writing prompts, copy of Pay It Forward DVD, and **Movie Reponses Questions: Pay It Forward** (pp. 90–98 in the Student Writing Companion), markers, colored pencils, desired additional art supplies*

Lesson Vocabulary

achievement n., a result gained by effort

legacy n., anything handed down from the past, as from an ancestor; something left behind

success n., favorable or desired outcome

PREPARE IN ADVANCE
*Complete a **Map of Your Dreams** worksheet to use as an example.*

FACILITATOR NOTE
This lesson is substantial and may take a full session. If you finish Activity One before the end of the first session, you can begin the Writing Workshop on the first day and complete it on the second. You may need to plan for three full sessions to complete Activity One, the Writing Workshop, and the movie viewing and response questions.

 ## WARM-UP :: IMAGINE WORKSHEET

- Refer students to the **Imagine** worksheet.
- Ask participants to close their eyes and imagine that they are twenty-five years old. Who are they with? Where do they work? Add any other guided visualization questions that are appropriate for your group.

- Explain to participants that they are to complete the worksheet from the perspective of their twenty-five-year-old selves.
- Once participants have completed their worksheets, they may either present individually to the group as a whole or partner up and stage interviews where one participant reads the questions and the other participant replies with her recorded answers.

 ## PROCESSING QUESTIONS

1. *What was it like to imagine yourself as a twenty-five-year-old?*
2. *Were you surprised by any of your fellow HERstory members' answers?*
3. *What advice stood out as being important to become successful?*
4. *How does your performance in middle school and high school contribute to future success?*
5. *What does success mean to you: personal satisfaction, money, power, fame, or recognition?*
6. *What can you do today that will contribute to your future success?*

 ## ACTIVITY ONE :: MY ROAD LESS TRAVELED

Part 1: The Road Not Taken
- Refer students to **"The Road Not Taken"** by Robert Frost in their *Student Writing Companions*.
- Read the poem and discuss its meaning stanza by stanza.

 ## DISCUSSION QUESTIONS

1. *What do you find hard about following your dreams? What do you find easy about following your dreams?*
2. *Have you ever felt that your dreams take you in a different direction than the people around you?*
3. *Different people may take very different paths to end up in the same place. Do you agree or disagree with this statement? Why?*
4. *What does it mean to be a trailblazer?*
5. *What would be the benefit of taking the road less traveled?*

Part 2: Map of Your Dreams
- Hand out art supplies and refer students to the **Map of Your Dreams** worksheet.
- Show participants your own prepared map.
- Ask participants to create—using words, symbols, colors, and images of their own "road less traveled"—a map of what it would look like if they carved their own path to follow their dreams.
- Introduce the word "legacy" and ask students to brainstorm its meaning.
- Review the Lesson Vocabulary definition of "legacy."
- Explain that as participants are creating their maps, they should remain aware of also portraying the legacy that they would like to leave behind.
- Give students approximately thirty minutes to complete their maps, or modify the time given to meet the needs of the group.
- Have students stand silently in a circle for two minutes holding their **Map of Your Dreams** worksheets so the rest of the circle can observe their work.

- *Option:* Alternatively, the group may stand for the duration of a facilitator-selected song.

PROCESSING QUESTIONS

1. *What did it feel like to create a map of your dreams?*
2. *What did you notice about each other's maps? Were there more similarities or differences?*
3. *Is it important to have a unique contribution?*
4. *Can you still be unique within a group?*
5. *Why would we want to consider now the legacy we want to leave?*
6. *What does "making an impact on the world" mean to you?*
7. *Why is it important not only to consider what is ahead but also what we leave behind?*
8. *What is one way you can make a positive mark on the world?*

CLOSING :: WHIP-AROUND

- What is one unique contribution that you make to groups that you're a part of?

ACTIVITY TWO :: WRITING WORKSHOP: LEGACY

- Make copies of the appropriate **Legacy** writing prompts at the end of this lesson.
- Give the students some time to write responses to the questions on the handouts.

ACTIVITY THREE :: MOVIE VIEWING AND RESPONSE

- Show the movie *Pay It Forward* to the class or substitute a movie of your choosing on the theme of legacy.
- Have the class respond to the **Movie Response Questions**.

SAY MORE :: ADDITIONAL WRITING PROMPTS

If time permits, encourage participants to write more in depth by asking them to write responses to the following questions.

» Whose legacy do you admire?

» Why is it important to think about the legacy we want to leave the world?

» What steps can you take in your life now to contribute to the world in a positive way?

Imagine

Please answer the following questions from the point of view of the character you are creating:

1. What is your name?

2. Where do you live (city and state/country)?

3. What is your job/career title?

4. How long have you worked in this industry or field?

5. What does "success" mean to you?

6. What did you do in high school that contributed to your success?

7. How did academic achievement in high school help you to become successful?

8. Why do you think you are successful?

9. What advice would you give to high school students who want to be successful in the future?

The Road Not Taken

By Robert Frost

Two roads diverged in a yellow wood,
And sorry I could not travel both
And be one traveler, long I stood
And looked down one as far as I could
To where it bent in the undergrowth;

Then took the other, as just as fair,
And having perhaps the better claim,
Because it was grassy and wanted wear;
Though as for that the passing there
Had worn them really about the same,

And both that morning equally lay
In leaves no step had trodden black.
Oh, I kept the first for another day!
Yet knowing how way leads on to way,
I doubted if I should ever come back.

I shall be telling this with a sigh
Somewhere ages and ages hence:
Two roads diverged in a wood, and I—
I took the one less traveled by,
And that has made all the difference.

Map of Your Dreams

Writing Workshop Part Seven

Legacy

1. Describe something about the world around you that you would like to improve and explain why. Tell how improving it would affect the world.

2. If you became famous tomorrow, what is something that you would like the world to know about the real you?

3. After you have lived a full life, what do you think will be the three things that you will want the world to remember about you?

4. Write a letter to your future granddaughter telling her in detail about the most important lessons that you have learned about being a woman in this world.

NAME

5. What does the word "legend" mean to you? What is a personal legend?

6. Tell the story of why the world has never been the same since you came into it. What makes you unique? What can you contribute/ give to the world that nobody else can?

7. Why is it so important for young women to have a voice?

8. What does it feel like for a young woman like you to free her voice?

Movie Response Questions

Pay It Forward

1. What values do you think Trevor stood for? What values do you stand for?

2. What do you think Trevor will be remembered for? What do you want to be remembered for?

4. Trevor created a movement that left a legacy that will affect the world long after his passing. What was the key element of his legacy?

5. How would you describe the concept of "pay it forward"? What effects do you think a movement like this would have on your community?

6. Do you think it is important to create change in the world? Explain.

7. Chris Chandler reported on the Pay It Forward movement that Trevor started, and thus his legacy only grew. Why is it important to learn about the legacy of those who came before us?

Part Three
Creative Output

"Creativity takes courage."
—*Henri Matisse*

"Theatre was created to tell the truth about life."
—*Anonymous*

Creative Output

Section Guide

The Creative Output section of the curriculum is the culmination of the efforts of curricular lessons and writing exercises to explore and cultivate the voice of the individual and collective members of HERstory. There are two Creative Output tracks that can be taken in this curriculum: a Literary Journal or an Ethnographic Theater Performance. The journal and performance are not mutually exclusive; there is a precedent for creating both when time and resources permit. We recommend contacting The Leadership Program for further coaching (see Reference section). It is vital to plan accordingly with your site. Please refer to the Creative Output Options Checklist in the Reference section at the back of this book to help guide your selection process.

LITERARY JOURNAL TRACK

YOUR PARTICIPANTS

Assigning Roles: You have had ample time to get to know your participants' strengths and proclivities. Assign roles for producing the journal; take into account not only participants' strengths but also areas in which you want to encourage their growth. Roles can include: the design team, responsible for aesthetic choices, general layout, and page design; typists, responsible for inputting the work into the computers; editors, responsible for proofreading inputted work and contributing to the layout; writing coaches, responsible for helping other participants improve the clarity, nuance, or tone of their own work; visual artists, responsible for continuing to create artwork and design various aspects of the journal, etcetera.

Democratic Design Choices: As you create your journal, ensure that all your participants have the opportunity to give input on the aesthetic of the book. Are you going for a scrapbooking style? Is the look traditional, or modern and sleek? Are participants going to self-generate all the artwork, or are you going to use clip art and computer graphics? These choices can be settled via discussion, vote, or any other appropriate and equitable means for your group.

Photographic Documentation: Photographs are a great enhancement for the book. Ensure that you have saved photographs from field trips and regular class activities, and perhaps even take photos of the artistic process of creating the book. You may also ask participants to provide you with copies of their own group-related photographs. One suggested method of obtaining these photographs would be to create an e-mail account dedicated to the HERstory Literary Journal, where participants may send their photos. Make certain that all students have given permission for their work and photos of themselves to be published, and refer back to your original permission slips for verification.

YOUR SPACE

Resources and Supplies: First assess what supplies and resources you have access to before making final stylistic decisions. For example, are you able to obtain and use computers, art supplies, scrapbooking materials, adequate working space, etcetera? As mentioned above, the Reference section checklist is constructed to help you make this choice.

Consistency of Norms/Code and Rituals: As you navigate the parameters of your new creative production space, it is important that new respect rituals are developed and old ones upheld. For example, if you are working in a computer lab, what are the policies and protocols that you adapt and follow to care for the machines and the work being saved on them? How do you ensure that there is still room within your working space for participants to gather in a circle for Rose and Thorn and possible kinesthetic activities as needed? If you have moved to a new space, where is the HERstory Code posted for easy reference?

Consistent Ambiance: Even under the circumstances of possible changes within your space, it is important that care is taken to maintain an ambiance that is conducive to the tasks at hand. Pay attention to developing music playlists that correspond well to the various tasks and consider altering lighting to fit the mood of the task.

YOUR PREPARATION

Determining Your Group Aesthetic: Before moving forward with your Creative Output project, it is vital that your group has a unified vision of what the aesthetic of it will be. The lesson What's Our Style? offers participants the opportunity to identify symbols and language that they feel is a fair representation of their individual and collective identities, and activities in the lesson are designed to help identify and clarify the meaning of the aesthetics that they will use in their final creative project. The cohesiveness that results from a shared aesthetic vision will allow your group to function more efficiently and productively throughout the creative process.

Literary Journal Creation Warm-Up Lesson: If your HERstory implementation is utilizing the Literary Journal Track, the acting lessons can be disregarded and in their place you should facilitate the What Do I Stand For? Collage Poem lesson. The artistic product that is a result of this lesson will ensure that all your participants have a visual art piece represented in the forthcoming Literary Journal. This activity will also serve as a kinesthetic and intellectual warm-up for the artistic process of journal creation that is to follow.

Literary Journal Generation: The Art of Words lesson will help you create your own Literary Journal. Using the seven themes above as Literary Journal section guidelines, choose from among the various writings the girls have generated throughout HERstory and the artwork they produced during the seven sessions of this lesson to design the Literary Journal. Be sure to include every girls' voice and artistic contribution in balanced proportion. To see sample pages of previous HERstory Literary Journals, contact The Leadership Program at: HERstory@tlpnyc.com.

Standards and Style: You may want a group review of the writing prompts results to discuss the standards and style that are appropriate for a Literary Journal. This promotes participant ownership in the creation and editing process and can lead to a round of edits/improvements to make the style of answers more applicable to a Literary Journal (e.g., convert a statement into a poem). Also note that if participants' writing responses to a certain thematic section are a little thin, their words, phrases, and poem stanzas can be amassed into group poems that credit several authors.

Assigning Tasks: Once you have assigned roles to your participants, the following task-based questions should be asked, keeping in mind available resources, time constraints, and participant skill sets:

- How is the work being inputted? Is it being typed into one file?
- Are participants e-mailing the facilitator the work? If so, does the facilitator input it, or the participants?
- Are there several participant typists who work during class?
- Who are the first-round editors?
- Which participants are generating additional artwork as it becomes necessary to enhance certain sections or entries?

Answers to these types of questions dictate how the activities that generate the journal will proceed. Further, these activities also enforce a level of accountability and protocol among the participants, preventing a rushed completion of the project and allowing for leadership roles to emerge within the group.

Noteworthy Journal Additions: Throughout the course of the program, your participants have already created several artistic/poetic pieces. Independent of the writing prompts, these are found in the Community Building or Writing Workshop lessons (e.g., Personal Values Posters, Name Drawings, Who's the Woman?, Body Intelligence, Map of Your Dreams, Around My Way, Show Your Pride). The creative products from these lessons offer an alternative avenue for participants who struggle with creative writing, enabling a more accessible voice within the journal for them.

Final Lesson: The Closing Rituals lesson is constructed with modifications for either track. Please note and follow the Literary Journal Track version. This lesson is to be facilitated on your final day of programming as your Closing Ceremony for the club.

ETHNOGRAPHIC THEATER PERFORMANCE TRACK

YOUR PARTICIPANTS

Ensemble/Cast Member Responsibilities: Each cast member must not only be responsible for their own part but must take a role in the support of the ensemble. Depending on the needs and aesthetic of your production, these roles can include but are not limited to: musical election—participants can research, select, and time the musical tracks/songs that will be used throughout the production; choreography/blocking—the participants who are kinesthetically inclined can lend their opinion and influence to blocking or possible integrated choreography; set design—participants who enjoy visual arts can contribute to the set and lighting design; or hair and makeup—participants who are so inclined can head the makeup and hair team to give their fellow HERstory members style tips and technical assistance in channeling their individuality on the day of the show.

Stage Crew: There may be HERstory participants who are not comfortable with performing onstage but have been active participants throughout the entire experience. These participants may be excellent candidates for the stage crew. Stage crew roles can include light and sound assistants, assistant stage managers, prop assistants, and assistant directors. These roles are crucial to the successful execution of the rehearsal and performance process. Establishing a stage crew early is an excellent opportunity for the participants to understand that a performance has many critical working parts beyond its actors.

Casting: Explain to participants that unlike traditional theater, ethnographic theater offers actors the chance to participate in casting themselves. This occurs through the use of participant writing to create the script. The more the participants write during the Writing Workshop phase, the more the facilitator will have to work with when generating roles/voices within the script. The poems and other parts of the Script Template that are not generated by the participants (e.g., "You've heard history; now we are going to tell you HERstory!") can be assigned based on merit and fit. They also can be used as incentives for memorization, positive behavior, etcetera, by delaying the assignment of those roles until the girls have "earned" them.

Costumes: HERstory costumes traditionally consist of a HERstory T-shirt with the HERstory logo emblazoned on the front and the girl's name on the back. Depending on your budget, you can purchase blank T-shirts and create them as a group project or order them from an online T-shirt customizer. "Flair" such as fancy lettering, glitter, musical symbols—anything that personalizes them to reflect the group aesthetic—can be added based on the preferences of the participants. The group can choose the colors for the T-shirts. The facilitator can then decide whether the girls should wear black pants, jeans, leggings and skirts, etcetera. The concept is to regulate the basics of a HERstory shirt and matching bottoms, while allowing the girls to individualize and personalize the rest of their ensemble with color and style of shoes, adding a belt or other accessories, choice of jewelry, hairstyles and makeup, etcetera.

YOUR SPACE

Performance Space: The careful choice of venue for performance is integral to the success of the HERstory model. You can select a space within your regular venue that is conducive to a performance or an outside venue that meets your staging needs.

Rehearsal Time: Whether you choose an external or internal venue, it is imperative that the full ensemble has adequate rehearsal time within the performance space. Acclimating your participants to their space is vital to their comfort and engagement, and ultimately their confidence. If you are thinking of using an outside venue for your performance, consider whether you're able to organize a series of rehearsal-related field trips to the venue before making your final decision.

Consistency of Rituals: All Opening and Closing Rituals should be maintained throughout the rehearsal and performance process. Adjustments can be made based on the particulars of the performance venue; however, the rituals are a central factor in the maintenance of the HERstory Code and the safe environment that has been created within your group.

Set Design: The set design is the key visual component in setting the mood and ambiance for the performance. The nature of the design affects not only how the performers relate to their space and interact with the message they are sending but also how the performance is received by the audience. After establishing the group's visual theme, colors, and symbols in the What's Our Style? lesson, devise a task list that includes collecting items for the set; determining what, if any, budget you are working with; etcetera. Once the items are acquired, roles and responsibilities can be assigned for prop care and set construction, design, and implementation.

Lighting Design: The lighting design provides an opportunity to complement the mood of the seven core thematic sections, such as use of bold, bright colors in one section, or spotlight only in another. Lighting design responsibilities can range from assigning students to assist with the light board to designing nontraditional lighting accents such as laying or draping of string lights around the performance area.

Sound Design/Soundtrack: In the Performance Piece, music should be treated as an integral part of the fabric of the story. Songs can be used for transitions between scenes and between core themes. Parts of songs can also accompany dance- or movement-based pieces woven into the performance. We recommend a preshow song list that loops while the audience arrives. These songs do not have to associate with a single theme but instead can include more general messages of empowerment. Choosing one or two of these songs to incorporate into your prerehearsal and preshow warm-up routines establishes a cohesive sense of mood and ritual. Allowing the participants to negotiate the majority of the musical selections will empower them to take further ownership in the full scale of the performance and will offer an additional platform for self-expression. If a participant suggests a song, be sure to listen to the entire song carefully to be sure there is no profanity or inappropriate subject matter. If a song is deemed inappropriate in parts but appropriate in others, you may edit out certain selections of the song or shorten it to suit the needs of the performance.

YOUR PREPARATION

Determining Your Group Aesthetic: Before moving forward with your Creative Output project, it is vital that your group has a unified vision of what the aesthetic of their project will be. The What's Our Style? lesson offers participants the opportunity to identify symbols and language that they feel are a fair representation of their individual and collective identities. The activities in this lesson are designed to help identify and clarify the meaning of the aesthetics that they will use in their final creative project. The cohesiveness that results from a shared aesthetic vision will allow your group to function more efficiently and productively throughout the creative process.

Introduction to Acting/Theater: Your students will likely have varying levels of theatrical exposure and/or experience. Thus, it is important to facilitate the entirety of the four Introduction to Acting Lessons that are provided in the curriculum. These lessons are designed to give participants an experiential understanding of the many facets of theater and serve as an ensemble-building tool.

Script Generation: Included in the back of this manual are a HERstory Script Template and Script Key. The Script Template includes suggestions of dialogue from original HERstory theater productions to start your theater piece and transition from one section to the next, recommendations for where in the script to transition between the seven HERstory themes, and ideas for choosing music to use under the transitions or in select moments in the script. The accompanying Script Key will guide you through the process of how to enter your own student writing into the Script Template to create your theater piece. You will find an electronic version of the script template to download at http://theleadershipprogram.com/script-template-code. The electronic version allows you to enter your script dialogue directly into the template. These tools will support even facilitators inexperienced in directing theater in the creation of a unique and dynamic ethnographic theater piece.

Memorization versus Staged Reading: A group decision should be made prior to the first rehearsal as to whether the actors are going to memorize their lines or whether the performance will be presented as a Staged Reading. If the group opts for a staged reading, then meaningful time must be devoted to discussing dynamic performance values and ensuring that the scripts are used as a tool and not a crutch. If memorization is chosen, that process can be motivated by giving the participants the script one section at a time so that they are not able to see the greatly anticipated next section until they have memorized the section in hand.

Noteworthy Script Additions: Throughout the course of the program, your participants have created several artistic/poetic pieces. Independent of the writing prompts, these are found in the Community Building or Writing Workshop lessons (e.g., Personal Values Posters, Name Drawings,

Who's the Woman?, Body Intelligence, Map of Your Dreams, and Show Your Pride). The creative products from these lessons offer an alternative avenue for participants who struggle with creative writing to have a more structured voice in the performance.

Rehearsal Process: Clarity of expectations is key for a successful rehearsal process. Rehearsal schedules and expectations should be clearly posted and distributed (e.g., the dreams section will be memorized by next Thursday's rehearsal). Parents, teachers, school staff, and the participants themselves should have copies of the schedule. It is recommended to rehearse the script by individual sections first and then in its entirety. There should be a separate tech rehearsal devoted solely to running the technical aspects of the show, including light and sound cues. It is imperative that a full dress/tech rehearsal occurs prior to the performance in front of an audience.

Postshow Q&A: After the curtain call, we've found it can be quite beneficial to facilitate a short question-and-answer session with the audience to allow the opportunity for a dialogue between the group members and the audience. For example, the girls get to hear the audience's immediate reactions, and the audience has the chance to learn more about the girls' creation and performance experience. You may want to end the Q&A with a special structured offering of appreciation to each of your cast members (e.g., an appreciation line where the facilitator offers each girl a rose or other token and states one way that she has been invaluable to the ensemble).

Final Lesson: The Closing Rituals lesson is constructed with modifications for either track. Please note and follow the Ethnographic Theater Performance Track version. This lesson is to be facilitated on your final day of programming as your Closing Ceremony for the club.

What's Our Style?

OBJECTIVE
Participants will identify symbols and language that they feel are a fair representation of their individual and collective identities.

SUMMARY
Participants will contribute to an object brainstorm, group poem, and processing discussion designed to help identify and clarify the meaning of the aesthetics that they will use in their final creative project.

AIM
How can this HERstory community best represent itself in a final creative project?

STANDARDS
CCSS – RI.7, W.4, SL.1, SL.2, SL.4, L.6
SEL – Self-Awareness, Social Awareness, Relationship Skills

MATERIALS
*paper and pencils; a box including but not limited to the following items: boa, fatigue head wrap, miniature baseball, football, soccer ball, basketball, compact mirror, lip gloss, glasses, briefcase, leather wristband, apron; the participants' completed **Who's the Woman?** list poems*

Lesson Vocabulary

aesthetic n., an artistic theory, system, or point of view

femininity n., the qualities pertaining to what is womanly

represent v., to correspond, stand for, or symbolize

resonate v., to amplify something that is true within yourself

FACILITATOR NOTE
Before this activity begins, ensure that the list poems from the Who's the Woman? lesson (see pp. 39–44 of this manual) are posted clearly on the walls of your room. The students will need to be able to access and reference them during the creation of the group poems in the following activity.

WARM-UP :: OBJECT ASSOCIATION BRAINSTORM

- Review the Lesson Vocabulary.
- Place the box filled with objects at the front of the room.
- Ask for one volunteer to be the scribe for the group.
- Explain to the participants: "We are going to attempt an 'association' challenge."
- Hold up one object from the box and ask the participants what they think of—what characteristics,

feelings, or any other associations that come to mind—when they see it. Example: A fashion magazine makes me think of glamour, beauty, the weekend, vanity, etcetera.

- Have the appointed scribe jot down what the participants call out.
- Continue this process until you have gone through all the objects in the box.

 ## DISCUSSION QUESTIONS

1. *Did any of the objects resonate with you? Why?*
2. *Did any of the associations that the group came up with surprise you?*
3. *If you had to choose one object from the box to represent who you are as an individual, what would you choose? Why?*
4. *If we had to choose one object to represent us as a group, what would it be? Why?*
5. *Do you have an object that you associate yourself with that wasn't in the box?*
6. *Are there any objects that we associate with the group that weren't in the box?*
7. *Why do you think some objects have more value to us than others? What imbues an object with personal value?*
8. *Do you think that we make associations about each other as people, just as we do with objects?*
9. *What are some associations that we have about women your age?*
10. *What are some associations that you wish people didn't have about women your age?*
11. *What are some associations that you wish people would have about you?*
12. *What are some symbols, tangible or intangible, that you feel represent who you are as a woman?*

 ## ACTIVITY ONE :: GROUP POEM

- Tell participants that they will now move to separate spaces in the room for a moment of reflection.
- Hand every participant a piece of paper and a pencil.
- Explain that they are to write about what the group just discussed in any format that they choose (e.g., poetry, free writing association, paragraph form).
- Tell the girls their writing must begin with one or both of the following phrases: "To be a woman with a _____ means . . ." or "Women who have/use _____ are . . ."
- Tell the girls the first blank space is to be filled with an object—either one object the group has already discussed or one of their own choosing. After they have written in their object, their writing can take any path they choose from the starter phrase.
- Allow the group five to ten minutes to write, depending on the needs of your group.
- When time is up, ask your participants to read through their writing and underline at least three words or phrases that resonate most with them.
- Pass out another piece of paper to every participant.
- Ask participants to write their underlined words/phrases on the new sheet in such a way that they can be cut out into strips.
- When they've finished writing, have participants cut out their text into small strips of paper that can be moved around like puzzle pieces to create a group poem.
- Divide the participants into groups of four or five students.
- Explain that their task is to create a group poem (a word collage) using all of their voices. To create this poem the participants should use their cutout words/phrases and at least five phrases from any of the **Who's the Woman?** list poems posted on the walls of the room. They

may use "linking" words or phrases to make their poems feel more complete.

- After the poems have been created, give every group the opportunity to share their poem with the rest of the participants.

- Have participants make a copy of their poem to paste into the Group Poem page in their Student Writing Companions (p. 100).

DISCUSSION QUESTIONS

1. *Did you prefer to write in a group or individually? Why?*
2. *What did it feel like to combine your words together as a group?*
3. *How did it feel to reflect upon the concept of woman in relation to an object?*
4. *Is a woman's voice more powerful if she is speaking as an individual or as part of a group?*
5. *What are the main ideas that you hear communicated in your group poems?*
6. *Do you feel like this poem is a fair representation of your group?*
7. *What does it feel like to have part of your identity associated with this group?*
8. *How can we maintain our individuality and make a positive contribution to the HERstory group? To other groups that we are a part of?*

ACTIVITY TWO :: IDENTIFICATION OF GROUP AESTHETICS

FACILITATOR NOTE

The following are suggested questions. It is important, however, that the facilitator modify the questions to suit the needs of the group.

- Tell participants: "We will now discuss how to represent our associations with being a woman, and the message we want to convey about being a woman through the aesthetics of either our Ethnographic Theater Performance or our Literary Journal.

POSSIBLE DISCUSSION QUESTIONS

Ethnographic Theater Performance Track

1. *We have established a set of symbols that we feel represent ourselves as women. How can we employ these symbols in our set design?*
2. *Why is it important that our set design is deliberate and intentional?*
3. *How can set design affect the way an audience interprets a story?*
4. *How can the set design actually be a part of our story?*
5. *While the basics of our costumes will be the same, how can we incorporate individual "flair" to visually represent our individuality?*
6. *How does the lighting design affect the interpretation of our story?*
7. *What colors do we want to use to light the stage? To light different scenes?*
8. *Should we use string lights or other lighting accents?*
9. *Are symbols used in songs? How?*
10. *How do our musical choices affect the way our audience will interpret our story?*

11. *How can we use our musical component to make our story more powerful?*

 **POSSIBLE DISCUSSION QUESTIONS**

Literary Journal Track

1. *What is our visual concept for the journal? Is it edgy, sleek, funky, bright, flowery, minimalist, etcetera?*
2. *How do we use our chosen symbols to define the aesthetic of our journal?*
3. *How do the symbols we use in the journal affect the way our stories are interpreted?*
4. *Why is it important to choose an aesthetic for our journal?*
5. *What would we like to communicate on the cover of our journal?*
6. *How should the cover art be generated?*
7. *Do we have a set color scheme?*
8. *What should the weight and texture of the paper be?*
9. *How does the way something feels affect the way it is interpreted?*
10. *How does our overall visual concept affect the way we decorate the individual pages?*
11. *How might the page design affect the way our writing is interpreted?*

 **CLOSING :: WHIP-AROUND**

• What is one thing you are looking forward to in the process of creating the Literary Journal or Ethnographic Theater Performance?

What Do I Stand For?

OBJECTIVE
Students will use the medium of collage to represent their values and what they stand for.

SUMMARY
Students will create poetry collages that represent their values using found words, phrases, and images from magazines, newspapers, and other media.

AIM
How can poetry collages represent our values and what we stand for?

STANDARDS
CCSS – RI.7, W.3, W.4, SL.1, SL.2, SL.4, L.6
SEL – Self-Awareness, Social Awareness, Relationship Skills

MATERIALS
writing paper, stacks of magazines of diverse genres, scissors, cardstock, art supplies, glue, tape

Lesson Vocabulary

collage n., a type of artwork in which different kinds of materials are pasted onto a surface to make a picture

ethics n., the accepted system of principles or moral standards upheld by a group

represent v., to correspond, stand for, or symbolize

symbol n., something that stands for something else; a letter, character, or sign used instead of a word or group of words

values n., the accepted principles or standards of an individual

FACILITATOR NOTE
Depending on the needs of your group, you may either have participants draft a version of their poem first during the activity, or encourage them to improvise it as they go along. Alternately you may bring precut, precategorized words, phrases, and images for your students' use. You may also want to create a collage poem of your own ahead of time as an example.

WARM-UP :: "WHAT DO I STAND FOR?" BRAINSTORM

- Opening Whip-Around: What does it mean to stand for something?
- Ask participants to discuss what the following quote means: "If you don't stand for something, you will fall for anything."
- Give participants a sheet of writing paper.
- Ask them to silently brainstorm a list of what it is that they believe they stand for. Refer back to the Opening Whip-Around and discussion to remind participants that they can stand for ideas, values, ethics, etcetera. Give a few examples if necessary to jump-start the brainstorm.
- When time is up, have participants pair up and share their lists.

- After they have shared in pairs, ask for volunteers to share with the group.

 ## DISCUSSION QUESTIONS

1. *Was it easy or difficult to generate this list?*
2. *Did you hear any common themes in what your fellow participants stood for?*
3. *Why is it important to know what we stand for?*
4. *How does it feel to stand for something?*
5. *What are ways that we can express what we stand for?*

 ## ACTIVITY :: "WHAT DO I STAND FOR?" COLLAGE POEM

- Hand out cardstock to participants and explain that they are now going to create a "What Do I Stand For?" collage poem.
- Explain to participants that by piecing together words and phrases cut from the variety of magazines that have been provided, they are to create a poem that describes what they stand for.
- Tell them that they can use single cutout letters, phrases, or sentences from the magazines and that the poem must be at least three to four lines long. They should glue their cutouts to the cardstock.
- Encourage your participants to make creative use of the space on their cardstock. Explain that their poems do not have to be pasted in a traditional linear fashion but could descend like a staircase or spiral across the page, for example.
- Tell participants that for this first part of the activity they are to use letters and words only.
- When they have finished their collage poems, instruct your participants to find visual images from the magazines to paste into their collage. Explain that these images should symbolize, complement, or enhance the words and phrases in their poem.
- Give your group at least thirty to forty minutes to complete this activity.
- Once your participants have completed their collage poems, ask the group to form a circle and have the girls hold their completed work in front of them in silence for two minutes so the rest of the group may observe one another's work.
- Have participants paste their completed poems onto the Collage Poem page in their Student Writing Companions (p. 101).

 ## PROCESSING QUESTIONS

1. *How did it feel to create your own "What Do I Stand For?" collage poem?*
2. *What was the easiest part of this activity? What was the most challenging?*
3. *Did you use a strategy to locate words and phrases? If so, what was it? If not, what approach did you use?*
4. *What made a certain phrase or image stand out to you?*
5. *Why did you choose certain visual images?*
6. *Why might it be important to find images that symbolize what we believe in?*
7. *Why might we be participating in this activity right before we begin production on our HERstory Literary Journal?*

8. *What strategies did you use in these collage poems that you can also use in the Literary Journal production?*

CLOSING :: WHIP-AROUND

• What is one word or image from your "What Do I Stand For?" collage poem that best represents what you stand for?

Literary Journal

The Art of Words

OBJECTIVE

Participants will create artistic expressions of HERstory themes for inclusion in the Literary Journal.

SUMMARY

The facilitator will lead students through the creation of a variety of visual art pieces to complement and accompany their written work for the Literary Journal.

AIM

How can visual art enhance the written work we have already produced for our HERstory Literary Journal?

STANDARDS

CCSS — RI.7, W.4, SL.1, SL.2, L.6
SEL — Self-Awareness, Social Awareness

MATERIALS

The Art of Words Guide (pp. 102–115 in the Student Writing Companion); the participants' completed written work (e.g., poems, letters, short stories); assorted art supplies, including but not limited to paint, colored pencils, crayons, construction paper, drawing paper, feathers, beads, photographs, and other materials of interest to the students

Lesson Vocabulary

juxtapose v., to place side by side unexpected combinations of colors, shapes, and ideas

represent v., to correspond, stand for, or symbolize

symbol n., something that stands for something else; a letter, character, or sign used instead of a word or group of words

visualize v., to make visible; to form a mental image of

FACILITATOR NOTE

This lesson consists of seven possible HERstory theme-based visual art projects that can support and complement participants' writing that will be published in the HERstory Literary Journal. Follow these project ideas and discussion prompts step-by-step, or use them simply as a source of inspiration for projects that suit your group. We recommend devoting a full session to creating artwork for each thematic category. Be sure to read the directions for each project at least one week ahead of time so that you can instruct students ahead of time to bring personal contributions such as photos and mementos, as needed, and so that you have the opportunity to create a sample project if you think it will be helpful for your group.

1. Identity

- Ask participants to brainstorm what internal qualities they possess and what qualities they like about themselves.
- Ask the group how they think others see them.
- Tell participants that they will create a reflection drawing that includes both their qualities and how others see them.
- Refer students to the directions for **My Reflection Drawing** from the **Art of Words Guide**

in their *Student Writing Companion*s, and distribute art materials.

2. Those You Are Closest To
- Ask students to visualize the people whom they consider family and whom they are closest to.
- Now ask students to think of a symbol that represents each person.
- Ask students to share some of the symbols and why they represent certain people in their lives.
- Tell students they are going to create a family crest, coat of arms, or logo based on the people and symbols they have come up with.
- Refer students to the directions for the **My Created Family Crest Drawing** from the **Art of Words Guide** in their *Student Writing Companion*s, and distribute art materials.

3. Body Image
- Ask participants to visualize a greenhouse full of flowers and houseplants.
- Ask them to imagine the smells, colors, and other details they would find in the greenhouse.
- Now have participants imagine a new kind of plant in their greenhouse, either made up of parts of existing plants or something completely imaginary.
- Remind students to visualize the size, color, shape, and smell of these new plants.
- Tell students they are going to create a drawing or collage of a plant that represents their physical self.
- Refer students to directions for the **My Body Is a Plant Collage or Drawing** from the **Art of Words Guide** in their *Student Writing Companion*s, and distribute art materials.

4. Love and Relationships
- Draw a large heart on a piece of newsprint.
- Ask students to brainstorm some things that come to mind when they think of healthy relationships.
- Write their answers in the heart.
- Tell students they are going to create individual collages that represent what healthy relationships are to them.
- Refer students to directions for the **Heart of a Healthy Relationship Collage** from the **Art of Words Guide** in their *Student Writing Companion*s, and distribute art materials.

5. Dreams
- Distribute a sheet of paper to each student.
- Ask students to make a list of five things they want to accomplish in the future on the top half of the page.
- Ask students to write down five things that they would like people to know about their character and personality on the bottom half of the page.
- Tell students they are going to create a drawing representing their present and their future worlds.
- Refer students to directions for the **Outside My Window Drawing** from the **Art of Words Guide** in their *Student Writing Companion*s, and distribute art materials.

6. Heritage or Tradition
- Ask students to visualize an ancestor of theirs whom they would like to meet or have a visit from. They may know what this person looked like or may imagine how the person looked.
- Tell students to imagine this ancestor brought a large container of some kind with them, holding the heritage or tradition that is being passed down to the student.

- Ask students to imagine what the container looks like, including the size, shape, materials, colors, handles if there are any, etcetera.
- Tell students they are going to create drawings representing the container and its contents.
- Refer students to directions for the **Delivery from an Ancestor Drawing** from the **Art of Words Guide** in their *Student Writing Companions*, and distribute art materials.

7. Legacy
- Distribute a sheet of paper to each participant.
- Ask participants to make a list of ten positive things they bring to this world (e.g., laughter, generosity, a good example to your little brother, love).
- Tell students they are going to make a drawing of the mark they are going to leave on this world using a thumbprint as an artistic convention.
- Refer students to directions for the **My Print, My Mark, My Legacy Drawing** from the **Art of Words Guide** in their *Student Writing Companions*, and distribute art materials.

 ## PROCESSING QUESTIONS

1. *What was it like expressing yourself by combining words and images?*
2. *What was it like to see the other contributions to the Literary Journal?*

 ## CLOSING :: WHIP-AROUND

- One thing I enjoyed or discovered during today's project is _____.

THE ART OF WORDS GUIDE

Identity

My Reflection Drawing

Create a drawing of yourself that focuses on your internal qualities. This drawing will include your portrait and its reflection. Make the portrait show how you think others see you, and the reflection show how you would like to be seen. The reflection can be in a mirror, a window, a puddle, etcetera. Use your imagination to envision where you might see the reflection of the "you" you want to be.

My Reflection Drawing

NAME

THE ART OF WORDS GUIDE

Those You Are Closest To

My Created Family Crest Drawing

Think about the people who make up your real or created family and those people who are closest to you. Consider what they mean to you and what each represents in your life. Design a coat of arms, crest, logo, or symbol that represents the people and symbols they've created. Include figures or words to show what the people in this family mean to you and how they are connected to you.

For the finished project, you may choose to draw the crest or coat of arms on a large scale that fills the paper and finish it either in color or black and white. Alternatively, you may use your imagination to incorporate the crest or coat of arms into a more detailed drawing (e.g., sketch the logo on a baseball cap, the medallion on a necklace or as part of the design of a piece of clothing that you are wearing).

My Created Family Crest Drawing

THE ART OF WORDS GUIDE

Body Image

My Body Is a Plant Collage or Drawing

Imagine that you have been asked to go to a greenhouse where houseplants and flowers are sold. At this greenhouse you can find any kind of plant, even imagine new plants — for example, a rose/cactus hybrid that smells like a gardenia. Pick out one plant in the greenhouse that represents your body. Draw that plant or create a colored construction-paper collage of it. Design this plant to showcase all that you like about your body. You may include words in the design of the plant as well. Think of the qualities of your body and try to give your plant some of those qualities. For example, if you like that you are strong, then you can design a strong and sturdy stem for your plant.

Next, refer to what you wrote in your body image writing worksheets and what you wrote on them. Now draw a tag for the plant that you just created. The tag can be hanging off the plant or sticking out of the ground near the plant. Ensure that the tag is large enough to fit care instructions for your body, referenced from the Body Intelligence worksheet. Your tag will include instructions such as: How often does it need to rest? How often does it need nurturing? What types of foods make it feel good? Does it need respect? Acceptance? Love?

My Body Is a Plant Collage or Drawing

THE ART OF WORDS GUIDE
Love and Relationships

The Heart of a Healthy Relationship Collage

Start by drawing a large heart on a piece of construction paper and cutting it out. Using magazines and pictures of your own friends and family, look for images that represent what you believe a healthy relationship looks like. You can also draw images and incorporate written words, if you prefer. Now collage the interior of the heart with the photographs, cutouts, drawings, words, etcetera.

Next, draw or use construction paper to cut out long twisting lengths of paper to create veins and arteries leading to the heart. Think of all the things that feed a healthy relationship, and fill those veins with words or symbols to represent them (e.g., trust, patience, understanding, fun). Instead of using words, you can use symbols to represent your ideas.

Your heart will now be surrounded by the representation of the vital elements of sustaining a healthy relationship.

The Heart of a Healthy Relationship Collage

THE ART OF WORDS GUIDE

Dreams

Outside My Window Drawing

Look at your list of five things you wish to accomplish in the future. Create a drawing that represents the inside of your room and that reflects your character and personality. Draw a dreamlike world outside the window or through a large hole in the wall or the ceiling of the room. In the world outside, create symbols for the five things you wish to accomplish. Use your imagination to find your own unique way to distinguish between the two worlds. For example, you might distinguish between the two worlds by playing with colors, juxtaposing black and white with color, or full color with a limited palette. Your choices should express who you are and your dreams.

Outside My Window Drawing

THE ART OF WORDS GUIDE

Heritage or Tradition

Delivery from an Ancestor Drawing

Imagine that you have a dream in which one of your ancestors visits you and hands you a very large container. What does the container look like? What materials is it made of? Does it have anything written on it? Draw this container in an open position so that you can see what is inside it. In it, draw the symbols, words, or literal representations of your family's heritage or tradition that have most affected who you are. Examples could include things that represent language, values, customs, etcetera. Remember this represents a dream, so let your imagination go wild.

Delivery from an Ancestor Drawing

THE ART OF WORDS GUIDE

Legacy

My Print, My Mark, My Legacy Drawing

Make a list of ten positive things that you bring to this world — for example: laughter, generosity, a good example for your little brother, love.

Then look very closely at your thumb to discern the shape of your thumbprint. Use the template provided on the following page. Complete the drawing by taking your list of ten things and using the words over the lightly sketched swirling lines of the thumbprint. You are thus using your words in the design of your thumbprint to compose a representation of what you believe will be your mark on the world.

My Print, My Mark, My Legacy Drawing

Introduction to Acting

Session One

OBJECTIVE

Participants will define "theater" and "acting" as a group.

SUMMARY

Through discussion and experimentation with different modes of theatrical expression, participants will examine their idea of theater and define "theater" as a group.

AIM

What is theater?

STANDARDS

CCSS – SL.1, SL.2, SL.4, L.3, L.5, L.6
SEL – Self-Awareness, Social Awareness, Relationship Skills

MATERIALS

*newsprint, markers, **Say More: Journal Exercise** worksheet (pp. 116–117 in the Student Writing Companion)*

FACILITATOR NOTE

A ritual of stretching, shake-out, exercises, and tongue twisters or chants should be chosen and taught at the facilitator's discretion to begin each Introduction to Acting lesson. Suggestions, which can be used in all four acting lessons, are included in the Acting Warm-Ups section in this lesson.

Lesson Vocabulary

The following definitions are applicable within the context of acting.

acting n., the art or activity for those who perform

characterize v., to mark or distinguish

conflict v., to come into disagreement or in opposition, a struggle or controversy

dialogue n., conversation between two or more persons, an exchange of ideas

embody v., to express, personify, or exemplify in concrete form

emotion n., any strong agitation of the feelings accentuated by experiencing love, hate, or fear; usually is accompanied by physiological changes

given circumstances n., in acting, what the author or playwright has given you to work with in terms of where you are, who you are, what you're doing, etcetera

improvise v., to compose and perform or deliver without previous preparation, on the spur of the moment, providing whatever is readily available

objective n., something that one's efforts or actions are intended to attain or accomplish; purpose; goal; target

physicality n., the physical attributes of a person, especially when overdeveloped or overemphasized

tableau n., a picture or representation of something

theater n., an acting company or dramatic performances as a branch of art

WARM-UP ONE :: ACTING WARM-UPS

- Tell participants that actors must warm up their voices and bodies before acting.

- Remind students to be careful in all their movements and to honor their own physical limitations in all activities.
- As a physical warm-up, instruct students to shake out one arm at a time and then one leg at a time, counting down from five. For round one (all four limbs), count down from five; for round two, count down from four, etcetera.
- Tell students to raise their shoulders to their ears and then let their shoulders drop three times.
- Instruct students to gently roll their heads to the left leading with their chin. Then tell them to gently roll their heads to the right leading with their chin.
- Finish the physical warm-up with a full body shimmy.
- As a vocal warm-up, tell students to repeat after you:
    - Red leather, yellow leather (repeat two times)
    - Unique New York, New York Unique
    - Silly spitting salamanders
- Increase the speed of the tongue twisters as students become more skilled at articulating.
- Include additional acting vocal warm-ups you know.

 ## WARM-UP TWO :: ZIP, ZAP, ZOP!

- Have actors form a circle.
- Have one person start the activity by making eye contact with another player and passing a hand clap to them while saying "Zip."
- Tell participants that the person receiving the "Zip" should make eye contact with another player and pass the clap while saying "Zap."
- Instruct the third player to make eye contact with another player and pass the clap while saying "Zop."
- Tell participants that the third player should make eye contact with another player and go back to "Zip."
- Have players pass "Zip, Zap, Zop" around the circle until a mistake is made, at which point the activity starts again.
- Encourage participants to pass the "Zip, Zap, Zop" as quickly as possible.

 ## DISCUSSION QUESTIONS

1. *What skills does this game require?*
2. *What role did focus play in this activity?*

 ## WARM-UP THREE :: I'M GOING TO THE JUNGLE

- Ask participants to sit in a circle. Instruct the first girl to make the statement, "I'm going to the jungle, and all I'm bringing with me is . . ." Have her complete the statement with an object that begins with the letter "A" (e.g., "I'm going to the jungle, and all I'm bringing with me is an apple").
- Tell participants the next girl will repeat the same statement as the student before her and then add her own object that begins with the letter "B" (e.g., "I'm going to the jungle, and all

I'm bringing with me is an apple and a book").
- Have them repeat the process until every participant has had a turn, with each participant remembering and repeating all the previously stated objects and adding her own object.

DISCUSSION QUESTIONS

1. *What skills does this challenge require?*
2. *Why is exercising your memory muscle important in theater?*

WARM-UP FOUR :: THEATER BRAINSTORM

- Explain to participants that in theater it is important to have a common working language.
- Record student responses for the following two brainstorm questions:
  - What is "theater"?
  - What does the word "acting" mean to you?
- Post responses up on the wall to be referred to as the acting lessons progress.

ACTIVITY ONE :: WHOSE SHOES

FACILITATOR NOTE
Depending on the needs of your group, for this activity you can ask all participants to be on the stage at once or divide them into groups of four or five.

- Ask participants to stand up and start moving around the room. Explain that there is no talking during the activity.
- Tell the actors that they are now going to walk "in role." Explain that to walk "in role" means to move the way you believe you would move if you were that character. Model a few examples if necessary.
- Possible roles include the president, an elderly man, someone who is very thirsty, a snake, someone who has a secret, a guilty criminal, someone who is moving along the ocean floor, a tired toddler, etcetera.

DISCUSSION QUESTIONS

1. *How did it feel to walk in character as another being?*
2. *What did you notice about your body in the activity?*
3. *How did you feel in relationship to other people in the activity?*
4. *Did you notice anything about the movement or expression of your fellow actors? Were the actors' embodiments of the same prompts similar or different?*
5. *Have you heard the expression "to walk in somebody else's shoes"? What does it mean to you? What does it have to do with the activity you just experienced?*
6. *What does it mean to embody a character?*

ACTIVITY TWO :: EMOTION TABLEAUX GUESSING GAME

- On newsprint create two columns. Title one "Emotion/Feeling" and the other "State of Being."
- Under the "Emotion" column, write one or two examples (e.g., angry, happy, excited, surprised, jealous, sad, bored, shocked, scared).
- Under the "State of Being" column, write one or two examples (e.g., hungry, tired, thirsty, itchy).
- Ask participants to define the word "emotion" or "feeling."
- Have them brainstorm as many different emotions as possible and record the results on the newsprint. Post it somewhere in the room for participants to refer back to in later sessions.
- Ask the participants to define the word "statue."
- Explain that they will be forming statues that represent different emotions.
- Explain to students that, in theater, the word we use for a grouping of living statues that creates a picture is "tableau." Model a few examples with one or two volunteers.
- Ask one participant to volunteer to leave the room.
- Tell the rest of the group to collectively choose one of the emotions listed.
- Instruct participants to individually create a statue of that emotion when you call out "One, two, three—action!" Have them hold their poses.
- Call the participant who has stepped out back into the room and give her three guesses to determine which emotion is being portrayed by the others.
- Repeat the process until each student has had a turn, or as time permits.

PROCESSING QUESTIONS

1. *How did it feel to create statues of different emotions?*
2. *Were any emotions harder than others for you to portray? Why?*
3. *What are the main giveaways that allowed the person entering the room to easily guess the emotion? Were they on people's faces? In their bodies?*
4. *Why might it be important in the theater to be able to tell a story just with your face or body?*
5. *What will you do physically on stage to tell your story?*

ACTIVITY THREE :: OPEN SCENES

- Introduce the term "given circumstances."
- Explain that given circumstances are the who, what, when, where, why, and conflict of a scene.
- Invite a pair of actors to the stage. Explain that they will be participating in an exercise called Open Scenes.
- Give each pair of actors a preset simple dialogue and a set of given circumstances. The given circumstances will dictate what the actor's objective is. Examples of dialogue:
    Actor 1: Yes.
    Actor 2: No.
- Tell the actors that the given circumstances this time are that the pair are mother and daughter, and the daughter is trying to persuade her mother to let her go to a school dance even though she is grounded.
- Inform them that the only line of dialogue that the mother can say is "No" and the only line of

dialogue that the daughter character can say is "Yes."

- Tell the actors they must try to accomplish their objective using only their given dialogue, but they may use a variety of emotional strategies.
- Other possible lines of dialogue for Open Scenes are:

   Actor 1: I have to go.
   Actor 2: But I want you to stay.

   Actor 1: You do this every time.
   Actor 2: It's not my fault.

   Actor 1: Why?
   Actor 2: Because.

   Actor 1: You're late.
   Actor 2: I know.

FACILITATOR NOTE

You may add to and amend the dialogue of the Open Scenes at your discretion based on the skill level and needs of the group. Be sure the two lines of dialogue are open-ended enough to allow actors to express a variety of emotions and intentions through them.

 ## DISCUSSION QUESTIONS

1. *How did it feel to work with a partner?*
2. *Did the introduction of dialogue make this activity easier or harder than the two previous ones?*
3. *How did it feel to have set dialogue?*
4. *Why do you think we did an activity with fixed dialogue?*
5. *What skills and tactics did you use to try to accomplish your objective?*

 ## CLOSING :: NUMBERS

- Ask group members to stand in a circle.
- Tell the group their task is to count to ten.
- Explain that they must count to ten without deciding who will say which number in any given round.
- Tell participants that if two people say a number at the same time the group must start again from one.
- Make atmospheric adjustments if helpful to enhance focus, such as turning off the lights, asking students to sit down, asking the students to close their eyes.
- Let students know that the goal is to reach ten. However, if the students exceed ten, they may continue and collectively make new goals for themselves.

FACILITATOR NOTE

This Closing: Numbers activity will serve as the Closing for all four acting lessons. This activity strengthens ensemble building and listening skills necessary for a successful performance. As the activity progresses, feel free to pause at your discretion and process the students' experience and the skills that they feel they need to be successful.

 ## DISCUSSION QUESTIONS

1. *What challenges did you encounter trying to complete this activity?*
2. *What strategies contributed to your success?*
3. *Why is listening to each other important in theater?*
4. *What strategies did you use to listen to each other?*
5. *What are the benefits of using listening skills outside of your theater work?*

 ## SAY MORE :: JOURNAL

- Encourage participants to reflect on their experience in the four acting lessons, and on what they are discovering and learning about performing, by writing on the **Say More: Journal Exercise** worksheet.

Say More: Journal Exercise

1. *Write about your experience in the acting lessons.*

2. What are some of your feelings and thoughts about performing?

Introduction to Acting

Session Two

OBJECTIVE
Students will develop individual and ensemble storytelling skills.

SUMMARY
Through ensemble work and hands-on expressive activities, participants will practice storytelling.

AIM
What skills do we need to bring the stories we tell to life?

STANDARDS
CCSS – RI.7, SL.1, SL.2, SL.4, L.3, L.6
SEL – Self-Awareness, Social Awareness, Relationship Skills

MATERIALS
*newsprint, markers, a scarf, one copy of the **Machine Checklist** worksheet per group, **Say More: Journal Exercise** worksheet (pp. 116–117 in the Student Writing Companion)*

Lesson Vocabulary

The following definitions are applicable within the context of acting.

climax n., the highest or most intense point in the development and resolution of a storyline

endow v., to furnish with some quality, talent, or faculty

ensemble n., all the parts of a thing taken together, so that each part is considered only in relation to the whole

personalize v., to make personal, as if intended for one's self; to endow with one's individual characteristics or mark

story arc n., the forward movement of a story, providing a rich and transformative experience

tableau n., a picture or representation of something

FACILITATOR NOTE
A ritual of stretching, shake-out, exercises, tongue twisters, and chants should be chosen and taught at the facilitator's discretion to begin each Introduction to Acting lesson.

WARM-UP ONE :: IT'S A CAT, IT'S A HAT

- Ask participants to stand or sit in a circle.
- Pass a malleable object such as a scarf around the circle.
- Tell each participant to endow the object with a different identity when it is her turn, and to demonstrate this identity in the way she handles the object. For example, if a student decides to turn the scarf into a watch, she might wind the scarf around her wrist and look pointedly at it as though she is annoyed that someone is running late.
- Ask the group to guess the object after each student's turn.
- If the group is having trouble discerning what the object is, encourage the girl whose turn it is to clarify her choice through more specific behavior, rather than by telling the others what it is.

DISCUSSION QUESTIONS

1. *What skills did you use to ensure that your actions were clear?*
2. *What did you discover about storytelling through this activity?*
3. *What elements of the actor's performances (e.g., her face, her movement, her words) were the most helpful in revealing the identity of the object?*

ACTIVITY ONE :: FAIRY-TALE TABLEAUX

- Divide students into groups of four or five members and ask them to privately within their group select a classic (well-known) fairy tale (e.g., Cinderella, Sleeping Beauty, Snow White).
- Review the term "tableau" from the Lesson Vocabulary. Remind participants that tableaux are frozen images, like a group of statues.
- Tell participants to create three or four tableaux in their group that they believe demonstrate the main story points of their selected fairy tale. You can give them the option of choosing a conventional beginning, middle, and end of the story, or of choosing the most climactic, evocative moments.
- Have each group present their tableau sequence for the audience.
- To prompt the actors to move from tableau to tableau, the audience will call out "One, two, three—action!" each time.
- Ask the audience to guess the fairy tale that each group chose.

FACILITATOR NOTE

A thought-tracking element may be added based on the needs of your group. Thought-tracking consists of the facilitator holding a hand over each of the characters in the tableau as a prompt for that actor to speak a sentence that conveys what her character is feeling at that moment. These tracked thoughts should convey the character's inner life, but should not "tell" the audience who the characters are (e.g., in Cinderella, "I'm so lonely. I wish I had friends to invite me to a party" but not "My mean stepmother won't let me go to the ball").

DISCUSSION QUESTIONS

1. *How was it to work within your groups?*
2. *Was it easy or difficult to agree upon the main points of your story?*
3. *What skills did you need to guess the other groups' fairy tales?*

ACTIVITY TWO :: TELL ME ABOUT THE TIME YOU . . .

- Explain that participants will be called up to the stage one at a time and asked to tell an improvised story based on the prompt "Tell me about the time you . . ." with the group filling in the specific instructions at the end of the phrase. Examples of possible prompts include: Tell me about the time you . . . went on safari in Africa, were elected president of the United States, attended the MTV Video Music Awards, landed a spaceship on the moon, starred in your own movie and attended the premiere, were given a million dollars to donate to charity.

FACILITATOR NOTE

The more outrageous the prompts are, the better, because it enables students to exercise their creative muscles and push the envelope of their imagination.

- Repeat the process for each participant until all have had a turn.
- At your discretion, prompt participants with leading questions if participants are stuck. For example, if a student was asked to tell you about the time she traveled to Saturn, you could prompt by saying: "I hear there was a very interesting life-form living on Saturn. What was it like? I hear the aliens taught you their language. Can you teach us a few words now?"

 **DISCUSSION QUESTIONS**

1. *How did it feel to be asked to create a story by yourself?*
2. *What skills did you need to accomplish this task?*
3. *What elements made your fellow actors' stories engaging?*

 **ACTIVITY THREE :: MACHINES**

Part 1: Preparation
- Explain to participants that, in groups, they will create living sculptures of real or imaginary machines. Each member of the group will step into a role as one of the working parts, or some sort of input or output. For example, if the students want to create an air conditioner, one can be the knob that sets the temperature, several students can be the air that is coming out, several students can be the water that leaks from the back.
- Brainstorm types of both real and imaginary machines with the class (e.g., a washing machine, a toaster, a microwave, a car, an elevator, a hair-washing machine, a banana-peeling machine, a laughter-producing machine, a shoe repair machine).
- Divide the participants into groups of five or six.
- Point participants to the **Machine Checklist**.

Part 2: Demonstration
- Instruct the groups that they are to choose one member of the group as the checker to fill out the **Machine Checklist**.
- Give the groups about ten minutes to create their machines.
- Have groups perform their machines in front of the class.
- Before a group performs its machine, ask the checker if the group completed all the tasks on the **Machine Checklist**.
- After each performance, have the class try to guess the name of the machine.

 **DISCUSSION QUESTIONS**

1. *What was it like to create a machine with your group?*
2. *Is it easier to tell the story of your machine and what it does on your own or with a group?*
3. *What skills did you use to come up with the machine?*
4. *Was it easier to create a real or imaginary machine?*

5. *Why is it important to be able to tell different kinds of stories with your body?*

CLOSING :: NUMBERS

- Ask group members to stand in a circle.
- Tell the group the task is to count to ten.
- Explain that participants must count to ten without deciding who will say which number in any given round.
- Tell participants that if two people say a number at the same time, the group must start again from one.
- You may make atmospheric adjustments to enhance focus (e.g., turning off the lights, asking students to sit down, asking the students to close their eyes).
- Let students know that the goal is to reach ten. However, if the students exceed ten then they may continue and collectively make new goals for themselves.

FACILITATOR NOTE

Feel free to pause at your discretion and process the students' experience and the skills that they feel they need to be successful.

PROCESSING QUESTIONS

1. *What challenges did you encounter while trying to complete this activity?*
2. *What strategies contributed to your success?*
3. *Why is listening to each other important in theater?*
4. *What strategies did you use to listen to each other?*
5. *What are the benefits of using listening skills outside of your theater work?*
6. *How will you use your listening skills as we prepare for our theater piece?*

SAY MORE :: JOURNAL

- Encourage participants to reflect on their experience in the four acting lessons, and on what they are discovering and learning about performing, by writing on the **Say More: Journal Exercise** worksheet.

Machine Checklist

Directions

1. Decide what kind of a machine your group will create. Examples: a hair-washing machine, a laughter-producing machine, a fruit picking and processing machine, a shoe repair machine.

2. Pick a representative from your group to be the checker. Your checker should go through the checklist to make sure you have completed all the requirements.

3. Let the teacher or trainer know when you are ready to share with the class.

Check each box when the task or element is complete:

O Every person in your group is participating in the function of the machine.

O Your machine has at least three moving parts.

O Your machine has at least three sounds.

O Your group has practiced your machine before performing it in front of the class.

O Your group has chosen a name for your machine.

Our Machine is called:

Introduction to Acting

Session Three

OBJECTIVE
Participants will develop their storytelling technique of "showing not telling."

SUMMARY
Participants will practice physical and emotional improvisation skills to "show not tell" a story.

AIM
What does it mean to "show not tell" a story?

STANDARDS
CCSS – SL.1, SL.2, SL.4, L.3, L.5, L.6
SEL – Self-Awareness, Social Awareness, Relationship Skills

MATERIALS
*newsprint, markers, **Say More: Journal Exercise** worksheet (pp. 116–117 in the Student Writing Companion)*

Lesson Vocabulary

engaging adj., tending to draw favorable attention or interest; appealing

improvisation (improv) n., something spoken or performed without preparation; something made or created by using whatever is available

nuance n., a subtle quality or difference in tone or meaning

portray v., to represent in a dramatic presentation

relationship n., any of various kinds of connection or association between people

unison n., the writing, playing, reciting, or singing of parts in a dramatic passage at the same time, or in a musical passage in the same pitch

FACILITATOR NOTE
A ritual of stretching, shake-out, exercises, tongue twisters, and chants should be chosen and taught at the facilitator's discretion to begin each Introduction to Acting lesson.

 **WARM-UP :: ALIEN**

- Ask four volunteers to come up to the stage and link arms to form a four-headed "alien."
- Explain that the audience is very curious to know what it is like to be an alien and that they have some questions.
- Have the audience ask the alien a series of questions.
- Tell the volunteers that the alien must respond to these questions as one entity. The students who compose the alien must form all their words in unison, listening to each other's nuances to decipher what word they are going to say next.

FACILITATOR NOTE
For reasons of time management or classroom management, you may choose to cast yourself as the sole interviewer so as to streamline the theme and content of the questions.

DISCUSSION QUESTIONS

1. *Was it easy or difficult to collaborate with your team members to become an alien?*
2. *What skills did you use to sense one another's speech and movement?*

ACTIVITY ONE :: RELATIONSHIP SCENES

- Explain to actors that, in the theater, one of the keys to telling a truthful and engaging story is to apply the adage "show don't tell." For example: jumping up and down and clapping your hands is a much more effective way to communicate happiness onstage than to just say "I am so happy."
- Divide actors into pairs.
- Give each pair a relationship in private, so that the other participants cannot hear what the relationship is.

FACILITATOR NOTE

The following is a list of suggested relationships. It is not intended to be comprehensive. This list may be adapted and expanded based on the needs of your group.
- *Mother-Daughter*
- *Father-Daughter*
- *Father-Son*
- *Mother-Son*
- *Brother-Sister*
- *Sister-Sister*
- *Brother-Brother*
- *Grandparent-Grandchild*
- *Doctor-Patient*
- *Lawyer-Client*
- *Boss-Employee*
- *Coach-Team Member*
- *Store Clerk-Customer*
- *Student-Teacher*
- *Husband-Wife*

- Lead a discussion with participants about the different dynamics that each relationship listed can have. For example, a mother and daughter can be so close that they can't bear to be apart when the daughter has to leave for college, or they can be in competition for who is the funniest. Each external relationship can have a variety of dynamics.
- Give groups ten minutes to devise a ten-line scene that "shows but does not tell" their relationship. For example, if the given relationship is mother-daughter, the daughter can say, "But Dad always lets me watch TV!" but cannot say "Mom, you are so mean!" The relationship between the two actors must be implied but not indicated.
- Have the pairs of actors perform their scenes in rotation.
- After each scene, ask the audience to guess the relationship and explain the process of how they figured it out.

 ## DISCUSSION QUESTIONS

1. *What methods of communication did you use to collaborate with your fellow actors?*
2. *Why is it important to "show not tell" in theater?*
3. *What role do relationships have in the theater?*

 ## ACTIVITY TWO :: FREEZE TAG

- Call two actors to the stage and assign a set of given circumstances (usually through suggestions taken from the audience).
- Ask the actors to begin to improvise a scene.
- Tell participants that when an audience member sees the two actors move into an interesting physical position or dynamic, she may call out, "Freeze." That girl then proceeds to the stage to tag out one of the actors and then replaces her in the scene, assuming the exact position the previous actor was in when "Freeze" was called.
- Tell the new actors that their responsibility is now to begin a brand-new scene with a completely different set of given circumstances that still justifies the positions in which the previous actors were frozen. For example, if "Freeze" is called when two actors are portraying a scene where they are playing basketball and one of the actors is in a position that indicates shooting a basket, the actor who assumes her position may begin a scene that involves trying to retrieve something off a high shelf.
- Repeat this process for as long as time allows or until every audience member has taken a turn.

 ## DISCUSSION QUESTIONS

1. *Was it easy or difficult to be the player who started a new scene?*
2. *Where did you draw inspiration from to create the new given circumstances?*
3. *Why is it important to create clear given circumstances in improvisation and scene work?*
4. *Why is it important for an actor to be skilled at improvisation?*
5. *Can you identify some of the skills that you use in group improvisation that are also useful when working in groups outside of the theater?*

 ## CLOSING :: NUMBERS

- Ask group members to stand in a circle.
- Tell the group their task is to count to ten.
- Explain that they must count to ten without deciding who will say which number in any given round.
- Tell participants that if two people say a number at the same time, the group must start again from one.
- You may make atmospheric adjustments to enhance focus (e.g., turn off the lights, ask students to sit down, ask the students to close their eyes).

- Let students know that the goal is to reach ten. However, if the students exceed ten, then they may continue and collectively make new goals for themselves.

FACILITATOR NOTE

As the game progresses feel free to pause at your discretion and process the students' experience and the skills that they feel they need to be successful.

 ## PROCESSING QUESTIONS

1. *What challenges did you encounter trying to complete this activity?*
2. *What strategies contributed to your success?*
3. *Why is listening to each other important in theater?*
4. *What strategies did you use to listen to each other?*
5. *What are the benefits of using listening skills outside of your theater work?*
6. *How will you use your listening skills in our theater piece?*

 ## SAY MORE :: JOURNAL

- Encourage participants to reflect on their experience in the four acting lessons, and on what they are discovering and learning about performing, by writing on the **Say More: Journal Exercise** worksheet.

Introduction to Acting

Session Four

Lesson Vocabulary

corresponding adj., related; akin to

logical adj., consistent in relation among the parts of something, such as a work of art

obstacle n., something that makes it difficult to do something

organic adj., forming an integral element of a whole; being an integral or fundamental part of a whole

FACILITATOR NOTE
A ritual of stretching, shake-out, exercises, tongue twisters, and chants should be chosen and taught at the facilitator's discretion to begin each Introduction to Acting lesson.

 WARM-UP :: HITCHHIKER

- Tell the group that this activity continues the work of showing, not telling, by using improvised dialogue and behavior to tell the story of who the characters are and what the circumstances are.
- Ask four actors to sit in four chairs that have been preset to represent a car—two seats in the front and two seats in the second row.
- Tell the actors that the given circumstances are that they are taking a road trip.
- Ask the audience to provide the actors with suggestions for what characters they are to play for the first round of the activity (e.g., a group of nuns, a group of cowboys, a group of Marines).
- Ask the actors to begin improvising a scene about their trip that includes their destination and the obstacles they are encountering on the way.
- Instruct the actors that as the exercise proceeds, they should pick up "hitchhikers" one at a time.

- Tell everyone that each time a new actor enters the car, the driver exits and the other actors rotate seats, so that there are never more than four actors in the car at a given time.
- Tell the audience that when a new actor enters the car, she enters as a new character and the group of actors then take on corresponding roles in that new circumstance (e.g., a group of cowboys who are going to the rodeo transform into a group of rock stars trying to make it to the show on time).
- If time allows, continue with the activity until all actors have had a turn to be the hitchhiker.

 ## DISCUSSION QUESTIONS

1. *What types of problem-solving skills were necessary to participate in this activity?*
2. *What skills were necessary for the group to perform cohesively?*
3. *What role does imagination play in theater?*

 ## ACTIVITY ONE :: GUESS THE SENTENCE

- Tell students that each girl will be taken aside and privately assigned a specific sentence, which she must then act out the meaning of without ever speaking the sentence.
- Send students out of the room individually or take them aside one at a time and privately assign them one of the following sentences:
  - I wish I could afford it.
  - I've never felt this way before in my life.
  - Why do these things always happen to me?
  - I wish she/he hadn't done that!
  - This is the most incredible day of my life.
  - I hate it when everything goes wrong.
  - What's the matter with you, huh?
  - There's got to be a better way to do this!
- Give each actor a turn to embody how someone would behave if she were thinking and feeling what the given sentence states.
- Remind the actors to use the techniques and strategies we have been working with in the previous three sessions, so that they can show, not tell, the story.
- Encourage actors to use movement and action as well as sound and emotion.
- Ask the audience to determine what sentence the actor was given from the improvisation.

 ## DISCUSSION QUESTIONS

1. *What tools does an actor have to communicate nonverbally?*
2. *What skills did you use to communicate your sentence?*
3. *What did it feel like to have to embody text without speaking it?*
4. *Which communication strategies were the most effective?*

 ## ACTIVITY TWO :: OBJECT IMPROV

- Call actors to the stage in pairs.
- Ask the audience to provide the actors with suggestions for three diverse objects (e.g., a watermelon, a cell phone, and a stapler).
- **Note:** The more different the objects are from one another, the more effective the activity becomes.
- Ask the actors to improvise a scene that includes these three objects in an organic and logical manner.
- Tell the students they must also communicate the given circumstances of the scene and portray their relationship.
- Remind actors to take a "show don't tell" approach to their improvisation.
- The scene is complete when all three objects have been mentioned and "used" through the dialogue and action of the scene.

 ## DISCUSSION QUESTIONS

1. *Why is it important to keep an open mind as an actor?*
2. *What skills did you and your scene partner use to accomplish your objective in the scene?*
3. *What does it mean to have an effective performance?*

 ## CLOSING :: NUMBERS

- Ask group members to stand in a circle.
- Tell the group their task is to count to ten.
- Explain that they must count to ten without deciding who will say which number in any given round.
- Tell participants that if two people say a number at the same time the group must start again from one.
- You may make atmospheric adjustments to enhance focus—turning off the lights, asking students to sit down, asking students to close their eyes, etcetera.
- Let students know that the goal is to reach ten. However, if the students exceed ten, then they may continue and collectively make new goals for themselves.

FACILITATOR NOTE

As the game progresses feel free to pause at your discretion and process the students' experience and the skills that they feel they need to be successful.

 ## PROCESSING QUESTIONS

1. *What was challenging about this activity?*
2. *What strategies contributed to your success?*

3. *Why is listening to each other important in theater?*
4. *What strategies did you use to listen to each other?*
5. *What are the benefits of using listening skills outside of your theater work?*
6. *What skills will you use to be an effective performer in our theater piece?*

 ## SAY MORE :: JOURNAL

- Encourage participants to reflect on their experience in the four acting lessons, and on what they are discovering and learning about performing, by writing on the **Say More: Journal Exercise** worksheet.

Closing Rituals

OBJECTIVE

Participants will identify and demonstrate appreciation for the accomplishments that they and their felllow HERstory participants have made throughout the year.

SUMMARY

Participants will create yearbooks to commemorate their experience and participate in several Closing Rituals designed to allow appreciation, commemoration, inspiration, and closure for the year.

AIM

Why is it important to recognize the accomplishments of the individual and collective members of HERstory?

STANDARDS

CCSS – RI.1, RI.7, W.3, W.4, SL.1, SL.2, SL.4, L.6
SEL – Self-Awareness, Social Awareness, Relationship Skills

MATERIALS

The Letters to Yourself that each of the girls wrote in the Welcome to HERstory! session (see p. 9 of this manual), blank journals with blank covers, art supplies, glue, tape, roses or yarn depending upon the ritual that you select

For the Ethnographic Theater Performance track, include a few copies of your final HERstory script on colorful paper, copies of any programs for the HERstory performance, decorations from your set to add to the ambiance in the room

For the Literary Journal track, include copies of the published Literary Journal, decorations to create the ambiance of a book party (e.g., special lights, a podium, refreshments)

Lesson Vocabulary

acknowledgment n., recognition of the existence or truth of something; an expression of appreciation

commemorate v., to serve as a memorial or reminder of; to honor the memory of someone or something

 **OPENING ACTIVITY :: HERSTORY YEARBOOKS**

FACILITATOR NOTE

Please see below for specific variations in the nature of the construction of the HERstory yearbooks based on whether the group took the Ethnographic Theater Performance track or the Literary Journal track.

- Set up the room beforehand so each girl can walk to her desk, preferably pushed into one communal table, where a blank book will be waiting for her.
- Instruct the girls that just as they have created their own HERstory script or journal, they are going to create their own HERstory yearbook.

- Ethnographic Theater Performance track: Give participants the copies of the script, the show program, the show invitations, and, if possible, photographs from the show. Let them know that they should cut out their favorite lines from the script, elements of photographs, etcetera, to paste into their HERstory yearbook in the style of a collage.

- Literary Journal track: Give them copies of the invitation to the book party, color photocopies of key pages of the Literary Journal, and, if possible, photographs of the Literary Journal creation process and photographs of the book party. Let them know that they should cut out their favorite phrases and poems from the color photocopies of the journal, elements of photographs, etcetera, to paste into their HERstory yearbook in the style of a collage.

- For both tracks, instruct the girls to create a front cover design and a back cover design, and to include the **HERstory Code** inside the yearbook.
- Once their front cover, back cover, and internal content have been completed, encourage the girls to invite the other HERstory girls to write in their books in the style of yearbook messages, describing what they have appreciated about the yearbook owner's contribution.
- Have the girls share excerpts from their books.

 **DISCUSSION QUESTIONS**

1. *How did it feel to create your own HERstory yearbook?*
2. *What were some of your favorite experiences of HERstory this year?*
3. *What were some of the surprises that you encountered this year?*
4. *Why is it important to commemorate your experience?*

 **ACTIVITY :: CLOSING RITUAL**

FACILITATOR NOTE

Depending on the needs of your group, select which ritual from the following two options is most appropriate to commemorate the HERstory experience of your group.

Option One: Rose Ceremony

- Have participants form a circle. Place two bunches of roses in two different colors within arm's reach.
- Choose a song from the HERstory soundtrack and turn it on at a low volume. Place this song on a loop so it repeats throughout the activity.
- Let the students know that this is one of the last times that they will be standing in a circle as a group in this capacity until the following year.
- Start the ceremony by asking the girls to cross their arms right over left and hold the hands of the girls standing on either side of them. Send a silent squeeze once around the circle.
- Take a rose in your hand, choosing one color to use first. Explain that these roses will represent something that the girls gave to the HERstory group this year.
- Hand each girl a rose.
- When the girls are ready, they will step forward and state what they gave to the group this year. After they speak, they are to place the rose on the floor in the center of the circle, starting a pile.
- After every girl has had a turn, distribute the other roses.
- Explain that this second rose will represent something the girls have taken away from the HERstory group this year.
- The ceremony is repeated as each girl steps forward, states what she is taking away from HERstory, and places her rose in the center of the pile.
- After every girl has taken her turn, explain that each girl is to collect one rose of each color. The first rose, representing what she took from the group, is to be brought home to commemorate her experience or slipped into the pages of her HERstory yearbook. The second rose, representing what she gave to the group, is to be taken with her to scatter all its petals along her journey home as a symbolic gesture of how she will continue to spread this attribute to the world beyond HERstory.

 **PROCESSING QUESTIONS**

1. What did it feel like to participate in this rose ceremony?
2. What types of emotions did you sense from your fellow participants during this ceremony?
3. Were you surprised by anything that your fellow participants felt like they gave to or took away from the group?
4. Why might we choose this type of ceremony to show our appreciation for each other and the group?
5. Why is it important to hold a ceremony to close out the year?
6. What is one way you will carry your experience with the HERstory group with you?

Option Two: The Human Web

Part 1: The Web

- Have the students set up a circle.
- Hold a ball of yarn while standing in the circle.
- Extend the ball across the circle to one of the participants, expressing your appreciation for what she has contributed to the group this year. This could take on the form of a trait, a value, or a specific reference to a time when she stepped up that was indicative of her character overall.

- Tell the students to accept the ball of yarn, loop a piece of the yarn around their finger, and pass it across the circle to another participant, indicating to that participant what she has contributed to HERstory this year.
- Explain that participants should continue accepting the yarn, looping it around their finger, and passing the ball to another girl.
- Tell the final participant to pass the yarn to you, stating what you brought to the HERstory experience.
- Take a moment to process the web of yarn that you have created around the room together.

DISCUSSION QUESTIONS

1. *Look at the web. What do you see?*
2. *Do you see any images, patterns, or symbols in the shape of the web?*
3. *What does this web mean to you? Ask the girls to take turns shifting their fingers away from the group, feeling the web move. What does this feel like? What does the movement represent?*
4. *Does the web remind you of any part of your experience in HERstory this year?*
5. *How have our lives become interwoven through this experience?*

Part 2: Keepsake
- Hand a pair of scissors to the participant on your right.
- Let the participants know that now will be the time that they are to share what they will take away from the HERstory experience this year.

FACILITATOR NOTE
This final activity can also serve as the closing Whip-Around.

- After participants state what they are taking away from HERstory this year, they are to clip the yarn a few inches from their finger, keeping approximately four inches of yarn for themselves.
- Have participants hold their piece of yarn throughout the process as the scissors are passed to each person around the circle.
- Tell participants that as they cut away their string, the others are to keep their positions as they had during the initial web formation—with their fingers in front of them—so the falling away of the web is visible to all.
- The facilitator should be the last to cut away her string.
- Let the participants know that this string is theirs to keep. It represents what they are carrying with them after this HERstory experience.
- Offer suggestions for how they can hold on to their string, whether it be to somehow attach it to their yearbook, tie it around their key ring, or put it by their nightstand or locker. It is up to them to decide where to keep this memento.

CLOSING :: LETTERS TO YOURSELF

- Tell the girls you have one last thing to give them before concluding HERstory for the year.
- Distribute to the girls the Letters to Yourself that each one wrote during the Welcome to HERstory! Opening Ritual.
- Allow the girls time to read the letters.

 ## DISCUSSION QUESTIONS

1. *What is it like to read something you wrote at the beginning of this experience now that we are standing at the conclusion?*
2. *Are you surprised by anything you wrote?*
3. *Was your experience in HERstory what you had imagined it would be? Was it different in any way?*
4. *Did you reach any of the goals that you set for yourself?*

 ## CLOSING :: WHIP-AROUND

- Read one phrase from your letter that represents a goal that you reached this year in HERstory.

Creative Output Options Checklist

If you need help in deciding which of the two Creative Output options is best for your residency, use the checklists below to make the determination. If time and resources permit, you may want to create both the theater piece and the journal with your group.

Ethnographic Theater Piece	Literary Journal
Do you have access to a performance space?	Do you have access to a computer?
Do you have access to stage equipment?	Can you offer youth access to computer equipment?
Do you have access to a sound system?	Do you have access to publishing software?
Do you have access to costumes or HERstory shirts and set decor?	Do you have access to scrapbooking materials and photos of the group?
Do you have the ability, budget, and space to hold additional rehearsal time as needed?	Do you have the budget and space to create the literary journal?
Do you have the approval of the site director and participants' parents?	Do you have the ability to make copies or otherwise publish multiple copies of the final product?
Do you have time to distill youth writing into a script?	Do you have time to distill youth writing into a final product?
Do you have knowledge of or a desire to learn how to create a theater piece?	Do you have the knowledge of or desire to learn how to create a literary journal?

Ethnographic Theater Script Tools

The Ethnographic Theater Script is a collage of writing taken from participants' Writing Workshops, music that is meaningful to the participants, and suggested components—poems, monologues, and quotes—that have appeared in every HERstory production to date, providing continuity and overall context. The template is applicable to middle school and high school level productions of HERstory. The primary element that differentiates one HERstory production from another is the inclusion of the original student writing selected from the girls' responses to their Writing Prompts. The Script Template and Key are designed to serve as a guide to the flow and logic of the show, as well as a source of inspiration for content and staging.

This section contains the tools you will need to construct your group's script. These simple tools are:
- tips for creating your perfect script
- a Script Key for using the Script Template effectively
- a Script Template (this manual contains a hard copy, or you can download an editable electronic version from the following URL: http://theleadershipprogram.com/script-template-code)

TIPS FOR CREATING YOUR PERFECT SCRIPT

- Spend ample time during HERstory sessions on the use of figurative language, poetic structure, descriptive narrative, etcetera in written responses.
- It is helpful to review your students' writing as it is completed and underline/highlight key portions of the writing for easy reference later.
- HERstory is a practice in which individual voices synthesize to become part of a powerful collective voice. As you compile the script, look for ways to highlight girls' individuality while weaving their stories together as one.
- You may also want to weave poetry or inspirational quotes in between the girls' writing.
- For each theme section of the script, consult with the students to choose music.
- Determine the proportion of the script devoted to each section based on the writing your participants have contributed and what suits them best.

SCRIPT KEY

The Template contains both formatting and coding to distinguish the different script components and margin icons for quick reference to find various components and sections.

Along with the margin icons you will find margin numbers that correspond to Writing Workshop sections. These numbers designate which text is to be inserted in the Script Template.

In the following paragraphs, number codes are listed along with their corresponding writing sections, and details about each icon are explained.

 You will find the music note icon in the left margin of the script where each music cue occurs. Suggestions for music are provided in the Script Template. MUSIC SUGGESTIONS WILL BE IN CAPS. Choices for where to include music and what music to choose for your performance should be based on the preferences and needs of your group, and how you want to complement verbal or blocking choices throughout the script.

 You will find a compass icon in the left margin indicating sample script stage directions. *Stage directions will be in italics.* As in all scripts, the stage directions are specific to the sample production. Feel free to follow these suggested stage directions or to make choices for your performance based on the structure, aesthetics, choreography, and needs of your group.

 You will find the "H" icon in the left margin where suggested dialogue universal to all HERstory productions occurs. **HERstory universal dialogue will be bold.** This dialogue has been successfully included in over seven years of performances with universal resonance among the various casts. The Script Template includes suggested opening and closing dialogues from these productions. You may make changes as appropriate to your group.

 Notes and suggestions for inserting student writing on the different themes and other original dialogue are indicated by a quill icon in the left margin, along with margin numbers next to the suggested places in the script to insert student writing. ***Writing selection suggestions will be in bold italics.*** These guidelines will assist with the structure and flow of the script and the creation of your original dialogue.

To guide you in creating an original script that flows, you will find, to the right of each quill icon in the Script Template, parenthetical numbers (#1–31) that correspond to the writing sections included here:

#1   Selected writings from Who's the Woman? poems
- Who's the Woman? list poem
- I Am . . . Poem
- Hold On . . . Poem
- Reflection Poem

#2   Selected writings from the Identity writing prompts that address:
- who we are

#3–9   Selected writings from the Those You Are Closest To writing prompts that address:
- friends
- family that we choose
- family that we are born into
- those we have loved and lost
- mother/daughter relationships where appropriate

#10–15   Selected writings from the Body Image writing prompts that address:
- perceptions of body image
- coming to terms with puberty
- negative and positive influences on their body image
- making peace with and learning to love their bodies

#16–21   Selected writings from the Love and Relationships writing prompts that address:
- what it is like to have a crush
- a first kiss
- thoughts on falling in love and broken hearts
- ideal mates
- healthy pledges to themselves about what they deserve in a relationship

#22–23   Selected writings from the Heritage or Tradition writing prompts that address:
- pride in traditions from their respective cultures
- influences of their heritage on their identity
- celebration of the cultural identities represented in the group

#24–27   Selected writings from the Dreams writing prompts that address:
- their futures and aspirations
- the qualities needed to identify and pursue their dreams
- their desired quality of life

#28–31   Selected writings from the Legacy writing prompts that address:
- their experience of finding their voice
- how they want to be remembered
- the experience of trying to affect positive change in their world

TIPS FOR FORMATTING THE SHOW

The format of the show follows the order of themes found in the Writing Workshops. Keep an eye out for responses from other *Student Writing Companion* sections that may fit well for a given theme.

Use your judgment in adjusting the length of thematic sections to reflect the quality and quantity of the girls' writing for each section. We find that different groups are more responsive to different sections. As you adapt the length of these original writing sections, keep in mind the overall arc and length of the show you are creating, as well as the balance you wish to establish between sections.

Music and Quotes

It is essential to keep the music and quotes relevant to participants of each show. The sample music suggestions reflect the experiences and sensibility of middle school girls in Upper Manhattan in 2010. It is important for you, as both the program facilitator and show creator, to guide your group's choices to achieve the same level of cultural relevance for them. Music, choreography, and blocking offer your participants excellent opportunities for further personalization and ownership over the collaborative collage of words and ideas that is the HERstory script.

Stage Directions

While some stage directions in the Script Template will be included in your production (e.g., the opening setup of planting girls in the audience to introduce the concept of HERstory rather than history), each production will have a structure and story of its own and will include variations in writing, choice of music, movement style, visual style, lyrics, quotes, etcetera. These variations will be determined by the style, preferences, and heritages of your community of girls, and will organically lead to the appropriate stage directions for your production. Feel free to use any of the structure and directions from the template that are suitable for your group.

SCRIPT TEMPLATE

Facilitator note: What follows is a printed copy of the editable electronic Script Template, which is available at the URL listed in the introduction to this section.

 ENTRANCE MUSIC SUPPORTS THE OPENING OF THE SHOW, STARTING WITH A MALE PERSPECTIVE OF THE WORLD AND SEGUEING TO INTRODUCE THE CONCEPT OF HERSTORY. (E.G., JAMES BROWN, "IT'S A MAN'S MAN'S MAN'S WORLD")

 The stage is empty with a single spotlight center stage. A girl dressed as a man enters from upstage right to entrance music.

 Girl One: Ladies and Gentleman. (*Clears throat*). May I have your attention please. History has many ways in which it can be defined. *History:* **A narrative of events from**

early times to the end of time. A chronological record based on real life events. A—

 The following girls who respond to the actress playing the man have been planted in two separate spots in the audience before the show begins. As they speak they stand up and reveal themselves as members of the cast.

 Girl Two: Um . . . Hold up . . . During all those events you speak of . . . where were we? Never once did I hear the word *woman* in anything you said.

Girl One: Um . . . As I was saying . . . *History* . . . Events, records that belong and remain in the past. An interesting past. A—

Girl Three: So you call women not getting the right to vote until 1919 interesting? An interesting past in which one gender dominated the government, the household, and the history book—

Girl One: Look. If you have something to say, ladies, why don't you come up here and do my job.

Girls Two and Three: *(As girls march onto the stage and usurp the position of the "man")* As a matter of fact . . . we will.

Girl Three: In fact, we already have been doing your job.

Girl Two: We've actually been doing it for a little while now, since, oh, I don't know, around about, the BEGINNING OF TIME!

Girl Three: So you've had enough of this tired old story.

Girl Two: Well, you've heard HIS-STORY.

Girl Three: Now we are going to tell you . . .

Everyone: HER-STORY! *(The entire cast of girls shouts this line from their various backstage/ hidden locations.)*

 TRANSITION SONG: IDENTITY

 Transition blocking for the Identity section as full cast enters the stage for the first time.

 (#1) ***Insert your participant responses to the Who's the Woman poem worksheet and a***

variety of different statement styles and actresses, e.g., a woman is . . . , a woman wants . . . , a woman needs . . . , etcetera.

(#2) Here you may insert selected students' writing from the Identity section of the Writing Workshop. Add writing where girls describe who they are, how they perceive how they are seen in the world, and how they wish to be seen.

TRANSITION SONG: THOSE YOU ARE CLOSEST TO

Transition blocking for the Those You Are Closest To section.

(#3) Insert your students' writing from the Those You Are Closest To section that focuses on the nature and power of friendship. You may insert students' individual shout-outs to friends here.

Here the focus of the Those You Are Closest To section transitions from friendship to family—both the family that they were born into and the family they have created.

(#4) Insert shout-outs to family here.

(#5) If applicable, you may enter a letter written by a girl to someone who has left her; guide the writer to ask for answers in her letter.

(#6) Insert writing that the girls have generated to pay respect to those who have passed on (whether from their blood family or their created family).

(#7) Insert writing about the challenges the girls face within their families.

(#8) If appropriate for your group, you may insert a line from one or more of the girls' writing that honors the contribution that their mother has made to their life.

TRANSITION SONG: MOTHERS AND ROLE MODELS SECTION OF THOSE YOU ARE CLOSEST TO (IF APPROPRIATE FOR YOUR GROUP. IF NOT APPROPRIATE FOR YOUR GROUP, SKIP THE SECTION BELOW AND GO DIRECTLY TO THE BODY IMAGE MUSIC CUE.)

Girls partner up and perform a dance to a song that they feel is resonant to this section. One pair at a time they break away and move down center stage and perform a pantomime of different mother/daughter relationship scenarios. e.g., Little girl getting lost and reuniting with her mother, mother teaching her daughter how to dance, etc.

(#9) *You may insert a series of lines in the form of a letter where the girls give voice to their emotions for their mothers, explain the impact that their mothers have had, and relay what they have learned from them.*

You may want to use the lyrics of a song or a poetry format to guide the girls' expression of their feelings for their mothers in this section, such as the "Caterpillar Song" by Miley Cyrus or the "M is for . . ." format of a line starting with each letter of the word "mother," etc.

TRANSITION SONG: BODY IMAGE

Transition blocking for the Body Image section. Girls call out a variety of scripted complimentary and insulting comments that young women receive about their bodies.

(#10) *Insert statements from the girls' Body Image Writing Workshop prompts pertaining to the pressures they are surrounded by that inform their body image.*

(#11) *Insert girls' writings on strategies for making peace with and improving their own perception of their body.*

(#12) *Insert references to those people in the girls' lives who have had a positive influence on the way the girls perceive their bodies.*

(#13) *Insert references from the girls' writing about their experience with puberty and how it affects the way they regard their body.*

(#14) *Insert statements from the girls' writing about how they are coming to terms with puberty and learning to accept and even love their bodies. You may want to use a poem along with students' writing, such as "Real Women Have Curves" by Alexx A. McCoy.*

(#15) *Insert final proclamations from the girls about the importance of self-love and acceptance from Body Image and other Writing Workshop sections.*

TRANSITION SONG: LOVE AND RELATIONSHIPS

Transition blocking for the Love and Relationships section.

(#16) *Insert participant responses from the Love and Relationships section of the Writing Workshop.*

(#17) *Insert statements that the girls have written pertaining to their experience with their first kiss or what they hope their first kiss will be like.*

(#18) Insert thoughts from the girls on what it is like to be in love.

 (#19) Insert explanations from the girls on what it is like to experience a broken heart.

 (#20) Insert statements that assert the girls' pledges to maintain their inner strength and integrity no matter what relationship challenges they are faced with in the future.

 (#21) Insert girls' descriptions of the traits of their ideal mate.

 TRANSITION SONG: HERITAGE OR TRADITION

 Transition blocking for the Heritage or Tradition section.

 (#22) Insert participant responses from the Heritage or Tradition section of the Writing Workshop. Insert several general statements of pride the girls have made about their heritage or traditions.

 (#23) Insert a section that represents each cultural group that is self-identified among your cast. This section has a very celebratory atmosphere—encourage the girls to cheer in support as the others are speaking and to attempt to incite audience cheering as well. Please note that "This is a story for the _____ woman" is repeated by the entire ensemble after it is stated by the featured group at the end of each cultural celebration section, e.g., "This is a story for the Colombian/African/Southern/Irish Woman," etc.

 TRANSITION SONG: DREAMS

 Transition blocking for the Dreams section.

 (#24) Insert participant responses from the Dreams section of the Writing Workshop. Insert several general statements that the girls have made about what they imagine for themselves and their future.

 (#25) Insert specific references the girls have made to careers and lifestyles they dream that they will have.

 (#26) Insert statements the girls have made about the quality of life that they want.

 (#27) Insert vows the girls have made about what they need and who inspires them to work to make their dreams come true.

♫ TRANSITION SONG: LEGACY

✦ *Transition blocking for the Legacy section.*

✎ *(#28)* **Insert participant responses from the Legacy section of the Writing Workshop. Insert several general statements that the girls have made about their experience of being women who are trying to make a difference in the world.**

✎ *(#29)* **Insert statements the girls have made as to why it is important for a young woman to find and use her voice.**

ℋ **Girl Four: I want to be remembered for making a change. For making history! I mean HERstory. I am a legend in the making!**

✎ *(#30)* **Insert the proclamations that the girls have made about why their legacy is important and why the legend of their lives should be/will be remembered. At the end of each of these statements, add the phrase "I am a legend in the making!"**

✦ *You may want to use lines from a poem such as "Phenomenal Woman" by Maya Angelou here with the students' writing.*

✎ *(#31)* **Add one final statement from the girls, asserting the power and strength of young women.**

✦ *One at a time, as they say their final lines, the girls take a step forward from their positions and walk forward to form a line in front of the flameless candles across the front of the stage. As they each take their place in the line, they join hands with the girl next to them.*

ℋ **All: I am a legend in the making!**

✦ *Final blocking as girls take position for their bow.*

♫ FINAL CURTAIN CALL SONGS

The Experiential Learning Cycle

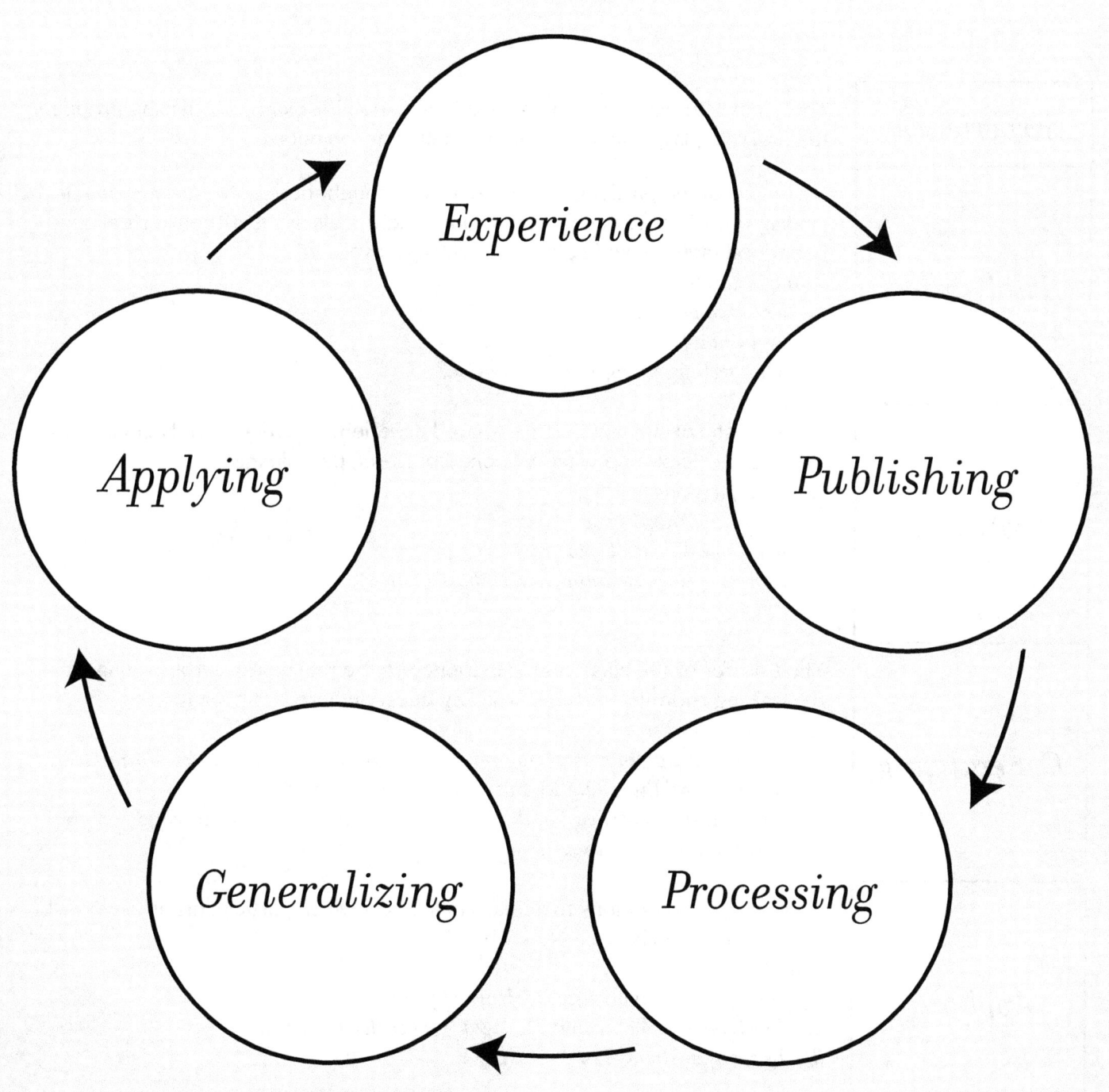

The Experiential Learning Cycle

Experience
Publishing
Processing
Generalizing
Applying

The "doing" to explore, examine, study, and identify. Examples: making products, fantasy, role play, planning, writing, creating art objects.

Sharing what the participants saw, felt, and thought during the structured activity. Finding out what happened within and to individuals at the affective (feeling), behavioral (acting), and cognitive (thinking) levels.

Example questions:

1. *What happened?*
2. *How did it feel?*
3. *What feelings emerged in the exercise?*

A systematic examination of the shared experiences. The group dynamic phase of the cycle. Exploring what happened between participants.

Example questions:

1. *What happened in your group?*
2. *What role did people play in the group?*
3. *How did people communicate with each other?*

The transfer of the classroom experience to the real world, extrapolating from the training room to "outside." The key question here is "So what?"

Example questions:

1. *So what general statements can you make about what you experienced/learned today?*
2. *What general things did we learn today in the activity?*
3. *Complete this sentence: "In the real world . . ." or "In the outside world . . ."*
4. *Why is it important to . . . ?*

Applying generalizations to actual situations in which participants are involved. The key question here is "Now what?"

Example questions:

1. *How could we apply what we learned to our lives?*
2. *In what situation in your life could you use this knowledge?*
3. *Be specific: "In my life, I can . . ."*

Classroom Management Techniques

Overview for Leadership Trainer: It is very important that the students in your classes understand your ideas of acceptable and unacceptable behavior from the beginning. Create and develop a definitive structure at the outset of the school year and follow through with it. Even though this program is based primarily on positive reinforcement, be prepared with discipline techniques. Here are a few ideas that can help you keep your classroom under control. Feel free to use all or parts of these suggestions or to develop your own tactics. Always include students in the process of creating classroom norms. Their participation in the process will ensure their investment in and willingness to follow the rules.

GENERAL GUIDELINES

Set Up Routines
Students love the familiarity of routine and ritual. While variety is important, inconsistency leads to confusion and lack of focus.

Establish Boundaries
Do a self-inventory and examine which behaviors you will and won't tolerate in your workshops. Think about what is important to you; it is very difficult to enforce a rule you don't truly believe in.

Respect Works Both Ways
Remember that as we expect respect from our students we always need to be modeling respect when interacting with them. This especially applies to the issues of fairness and listening; young adults are very sensitive to whether or not they are treated fairly and will be much more willing to follow rules and norms if they feel they are being heard.

Address the Behavior, Not the Person
If a student must be reprimanded for inappropriate behavior, make sure she understands that it is the behavior that is undesirable, not the student. Example: "You are welcome in this workshop, and you have a lot to offer. Your recent behavior is unacceptable, but we would like to have you contributing in a positive way at any time."

Don't Be Afraid to Be Firm

Inappropriate behavior deserves a swift and strong response. Don't fall into the trap of thinking "This student just needs time to adjust to these new rules and norms." Students will always test boundaries—at the beginning, middle, and end of the year. They need to know that the rules are the same for all students at all times.

Give Students a Share in Community Decision Making

If a problem arises, call a community meeting and ask for student input on how to solve it. This does not undermine your authority but will support it, as you will have students on your side, solving the problem with you.

POSITIVE REINFORCEMENT

Positive reinforcement can reduce the need for discipline. Encouraging good/healthy behavior helps students develop good/healthy habits. Use specific, descriptive praise so that the students are able to recognize the actual behavior and why it is good. Aim to acknowledge all good/healthy behavior; try not to let any slip by.

Star Charts

If you choose to use a star chart, implement the guidelines at the beginning of the year. Involve your class in setting up individual and/or class goals and rewards. Example: If a student receives five individual stars, a certificate of recognition is sent home. If the class receives ten class stars, the class gets a special day or has a little party.

Stickers

Give out stickers to reinforce good behaviors. Example: If the girl who never shares offers to share her markers with a classmate, respond with positive feedback and a sticker of her choice.

You may also want to distribute stickers at the end of the day. Make it clear at the beginning of class that those who demonstrate appropriate behavior—a good leadership quality—throughout the session will receive a sticker to take home; those who do not demonstrate appropriate behavior will not get a sticker. This system works only if you really follow through on consequences.

"What I See in You" Certificate

Create an attractive certificate to give to students who exhibit leadership skills. Example: "What I see in you is . . . you helped another student." You might also use this certificate to reward behaviors such as being a good friend, being cooperative, participating, etcetera.

Special Privileges

Create special opportunities for students who achieve important goals. Example: Allow a student who has shown improvement to lead an activity, tell a story, help the teacher, etcetera.

High Fives

High-five students who show progress or demonstrate a leadership quality.

Group Chant

Create a group chant or cheer of affirmation that you and your class can recite at the beginning of each session or before an activity to build a strong group dynamic. Example: "We are leaders, smart and true! We are leaders, how 'bout you?"

Good Behavior Medal

Make a round medallion out of felt, decorative paper, glitter, or anything else that would make it special, and string it on a ribbon. Choose a student at the end of each day who, because of good behavior or visible progress, will get to wear the medal around her neck during the next class.

DISCIPLINE TECHNIQUES

As with positive reinforcement, discipline techniques must be specific, clear, and followed through. It is important that the actions' consequences make sense to students so they are able to learn from their experiences. The most important part of classroom management is to establish at the beginning of the year clear rules and consequences and strictly enforce them.

Leadership Contract

As a class, develop a behavior contract that everyone agrees upon. This Leadership Contract can include such things as general classroom rules, reward systems, consequences for inappropriate behavior, a definition of cooperation, etcetera. Both your signature and each student's signature should appear on the contract. Refer back to the contract throughout the year whenever it is broken.

"Freeze, Simon Says"

If the whole class gets rowdy, tell them to freeze and touch their heads. Continue with different "Touch your _____" prompts so that the instructions lead into a short game (similar to Simon Says without the "Simon says" command). This will redirect the attention back to you.

Guess My Behavior

Call out: "Freeze." Make sure everyone is seated and hand each student a piece of paper and a marker. Instruct each student to write one word that describes what she was just doing. Collect the pieces of paper and put them into a hat (or anything that can hold them). Choose a student to come to the front of the room, pick a piece of paper out of the hat, and act out the word on the paper. Whoever guesses the behavior/action correctly gets to come up and act out the next word. After a few examples, have the class talk about what they learned from watching these inappropriate behaviors and how they can avoid them next time.

The Silent Method

At times, simply becoming quiet can send a message to the students that you are dissatisfied with the way things are going. Once they notice that you are not talking, they often become curious why and give you their attention.

If You Can Hear Me . . .

Another spin on the silent method is to get very quiet and softly say, "If you can hear me, clap your hands. If you can hear me, [fill in command]." Repeat this until everyone is participating.

Call and Response

Call and response is a great way to get everyone's attention. It confirms your role as the teacher and the class members' role as the students. Because the call and the response are equally important, this activity tells the student, "If our classroom is going to function well, we need to work as a team." It's also a fun way to let out a last hurrah before settling down. Teach your call and response to the class on the first day so everyone will know how to chime in when you give the prompt. Use these examples or create chants/rhythms of your own.

Teacher: "Boom, Boom" . . . **Students:** "Chica, Chica"

Teacher: "Zip" . . . **Students:** "Zap" . . . **Teacher:** "Zop"

"I Need Attention!"

Sometimes when students act out they are simply asking for attention. Give them a role or task, such as teacher's helper, or use their names in the story you're telling or directions you're giving. Example: "Amanda and Marie lived a long, long time ago . . ." or "Amanda may choose to color his house blue, and Marie may choose to color her house red . . .")

The Look

Staring at the disruptive students with a certain look or moving closer to them can give them the attention that they need and prevent their off-task behavior from swelling.

Silence Symbol

At the beginning of the semester, establish a symbol that will let students know that they need to be silent. Turning lights on and off, holding up your arm, or ringing a bell all work to achieve this effect.

Time-Out

Sometimes a student needs time to calm down away from her fellow students. Take the student aside and explain how her behavior is not helping the activity. Give the student time to sit quietly at the side of the room and watch the activity until she feels ready to join the group and follow the rules.

Theoretical Rationale

WHY HERSTORY?

Out-of-school time provides a promising opportunity to address the unique challenges faced by adolescent girls. Research demonstrates that participation in after-school programs during adolescence is associated with higher levels of educational attainment (Eccles & Barber, 1999; Mahoney, Cairns & Farmer, 2003), reductions in negative behaviors such as delinquency and drug use (Mahoney, 2000; Rhodes & Spencer, 2005; Youniss, McLellan, Su & Yates, 1999), and increases in psychosocial competencies that serve as protective factors against negative outcomes, such as self-efficacy (Catalano et al., 1999; Eccles & Gootman, 2002).

In addition, because most girls attend coed schools, out-of-school-time programming can provide a much-needed single-gender space for girls to address issues that are not or cannot be addressed within the school context. For example, girls experience significant media and cultural pressure to maintain an idealized image, and research demonstrates that exposure to and internalization of the sexualized and thin body in media is associated with poorer outcomes across a wide range of health and behavior indicators, including both physical and mental health outcomes (Marti, Stice & Springer, 2010; Grabe, Ward & Hyde, 2008; White House Council on Women & Girls [WHCWG], 2011; American Psychological Association's Task Force on the Sexualization of Girls, 2007; Impett, Schooler & Tolman, 2006). Contrary to stereotype, these effects are similar for white women and women of color (O'Neill, 2003). The causal pathway for these effects appears to be through several identity-related protective factors such as self-esteem, positive body image, and connectedness across domains, including peers, family, and school.

The adolescent years are also an important time for girls academically. Their downward trajectory in math and science begins in middle school as girls internalize academic stereotypes (e.g., that girls are not good at math) that compromise their performance (Spencer, Steele & Quinn, 1999; American Association of University Women [AAUW], 2001). Furthermore, while girls traditionally do better in writing and English than their male counterparts (WHCWG, 2011), there is still a need for significant improvement in this area, as US girls' scores for reading and writing attainment are below females in other developed nations. Advances are especially needed among girls who attend underserved schools where test scores are even lower than the US national average and certainly international standards (Ornstein & Levine, 2008).

The HERstory program is designed to promote positive academic and health-related outcomes for adolescent girls by targeting both individual and environmental factors associated with healthy development. As mentioned above in the program description, one of the primary change mechanisms for HERstory is its encouragement of strong peer relationships. Establishing positive peer networks, such as the ones encouraged within HERstory, is a protective factor for girls (Frey & Röthlisberger, 1999) and can guard against academic failure and substance use (Morrison, Brown, D'Incau, O'Farrell & Furlong, 2006; Willis, Resko, Ainette & Mendoza, 2004). Many of the initial sessions of HERstory are devoted to establishing supportive peer relationships. Community Building uses group bonding activities with both physical and verbal components to support the formation of peer connections, which are created through mutual self-disclosure (Buhrmester & Prager, 1995) and sustained through sharing activities (Fehr, 2004; McNelles & Connolly, 1999; Radmacher & Azmitia, 2006; Reis & Shaver, 1988). The Creative Output section also facilitates these bonds, as group projects promote teamwork and facilitate inter-group dialogue (Connors, 1998; Cooper & Sjostrom, 2006). It seems likely the bonds are all the more important because they are established in the safety of a single-sex space, leading to more open and expressive discussions between individuals than those that would occur in a coed environment (Maccoby, 1988).

Because HERstory is mainly implemented in schools, cohesiveness may go beyond the group, potentially creating bonds between participants and adults at the school; this is called school connectedness. Researchers at the Centers for Disease Control and Prevention (CDC) have identified school connectedness as a crucial protective factor in healthy development. It is the single strongest protective factor against violence, substance abuse, and school absenteeism, and the second strongest protective factor against emotional distress, disordered eating, and suicidal ideation (CDC, 2009; Resnick, Bearman, Blum, et al., 1997; Resnick, Harris & Blum, 1993; Nonnemaker, McNeely & Blum, 2007). The Creative Output section targets school connectedness explicitly by involving staff and other youth as audience members for the final theatrical performance.

In addition to building connectedness across domains, HERstory benefits youth through targeted social-emotional skill building. Lessons in the Community Building portion of the program help youth improve their communication skills by reinforcing basic conflict-resolution, problem-solving, and leadership skills such as perspective taking, active listening, and using I-messages. Increases in these skills are associated with improvements in self-esteem, self-efficacy, and identity development, all of which are protective factors that facilitate positive youth development (Eccles & Gootman, 2002). These exercises, along with lessons and prompts from the Writing Workshop section, build participants' intellectual development, including critical thinking and reasoning skills such as cultural competency and social awareness. In addition, many Writing Workshop topics target specific protective factors. Dreams and Legacy are both designed to promote future orientation, while Identity and Heritage or Tradition work to establish a strong positive (including ethnic) identity.

The creative process itself also promotes positive youth development. It is associated with increases in self-regulation, an analytic framework, self-efficacy, and positive identity development (Baum, Owen & Oreck, 1997; Fredricks & Eccles, 2005; Hetland et al., 2007; Philips, Linington &

Penman, 1999). Creative and self-expressive writing is critical for young women as it facilitates the development of their identities in a world where they are often defined by others' expectations (Gardiner, 1981). The free-form writing allows for creativity and self-expression that encourage individual reflection (Peterson & Jones, 2001).

CONCLUSION

Given the world that young women inhabit and the sensitive developmental time period of adolescence, HERstory is an ideal program for combating negative messages from the media and peers by creating positive opportunities for change in the school environment and encouraging the development of social-emotional learning skills in the participants. These changes foster protective factors in HERstory participants, including positive peer support, school connectedness, and self-efficacy; such factors give young women the resources to be personally empowered against the barrage of negative behaviors and stereotypes that might otherwise adversely affect their development and future trajectories.

Curricular Framework

As a research-based program, HERstory's curricular framework and materials are designed to utilize the best practices for promoting social-emotional learning. The progression of the curriculum ensures that skills are taught according to the SAFE framework (Durlak & Weissberg, 2007): lessons are Sequential and Active and contain content that is Focused and Explicit. Therefore, it is important to ensure that program facilitators follow the curricular progression laid out below.

Each TLP session follows a set lesson structure that includes an Aim, Warm-Up, Activity, and Closing. Within each segment of the TLP lesson structure, facilitators use the experiential learning cycle (Pfiffer & Jones, 1975, 1983), a structured sequence of activities that is designed to accommodate multiple learning styles and social group differences (race, gender, socio-economic status, and ability). More information about the TLP lesson structure and the experiential learning cycle are contained in the Facilitation Tips section in the introduction to this volume.

HERstory's curricular framework is designed to focus on the unique needs of adolescent girls. The program's three core components, Community Building, Writing Workshop, and Creative Output, build academic and social-emotional skills in a manner that facilitates identity development and group cohesion while promoting positive youth development. In the Community Building section, the facilitator leads participants through lessons utilizing both verbal and physical activities designed to foster group cohesion and develop positive peer support networks. Lessons in this portion include Human Barometer, an exercise where the facilitator reads a statement and youth move around the room to express their degree of agreement. This, and similar activities, help youth develop their critical thinking and reasoning skills, gain confidence expressing their points of view in the face of social pressure, and build trust and understanding among participants.

Participants spend the majority of HERstory's sessions focused on developing academic and self-expressive skills though writing exercises that give participating youth a designated space to explore aspects of identity during the Writing Workshop section. Structured topically, it begins with a two-session lesson on identity exploration (Identity), then expands to include two-session lessons on immediate circles of influence in participants' lives (Those You Are Closest To) and relevant topics for adolescent girls (Body Image, Love and Relationships). Girls are then encouraged to think about the trajectory of their lives in three segments that explore where they come from (Heritage or Tradition), where they want to go (Dreams), and how they want to be remembered (Legacy). The life trajectory section of the Writing Workshop is specifically designed to develop future orientation, encourage goal setting, and promote ethnic identity development, all of which are crucial protective factors essential to healthy youth development (Catalano, Berglund, Ryan, Lonczak & Hawkins, 1999). Exercises in the Writing Workshop include participation in a curriculum-based lesson relevant to the topic and opportunities to respond to thematically appropriate writing prompts.

In the Creative Output section, youth spend time learning about the process of putting on a show or creating a literary journal. Then, the facilitator crafts a script for the theater piece or begins to fashion a literary journal using the participants' responses to their writing prompts (as well as the script template and guidelines in the theater option). Participants performing an ethnographic theater piece spend their remaining sessions rehearsing the theater piece and performing it for a live audience, while those creating a literary journal develop their product and share it through a "book party." For both, some form of sharing with a broader audience is an essential element of the HERstory process; girls who are subject to numerous external expectations can develop confidence by telling their own stories.

Credits

Page 1 Ani DiFranco quote used with permission courtesy of Righteous Babe Records.

Page 83 Meg Rosoff quote used with permission courtesy of copyright owner Guardian News & Media Ltd.

Bibliography

Altschul, A., Oyserman, D. & Bybee, D. (2006). Racial-ethnic identity in mid-adolescence: Content and change as predictors of academic achievement. *Child Development,* 77(5), 1155–1169.

American Association of University Women. (2001). Beyond the "gender wars": A conversation about girls, boys, and education. Washington, DC: American Association of University Women Education Foundation. Retrieved 28 June 2011 from: http://cdm16064.contentdm.oclc.org/cdm/ref/collection/p266901coll4/id/2566

American Psychological Association, Task Force on the Sexualization of Girls. (2007). *Reports of the APA task force on the sexualization of girls.* Washington, DC: American Psychological Association.

Allen, J.P., Philliber, S., Herrling, S. & Kuperminc, G. P. (1997). Preventing teen pregnancy and academic failure: Experimental evaluation of a developmentally based approach. *Child Development,* 64(4), 729–742.

Arnett, J. J. (1999). Adolescent storm and stress, reconsidered. *American Psychologist,* 54, 317–326.

Baum, S., Owen, S. & Oreck, B. (1997). Transferring individual self-regulation processes from the arts to academics. *Arts Education Policy Review,* 98(3), 32–39.

Buhrmester, D. & Prager, K. (1995). Patterns and functions of self-disclosure during childhood and adolescence. In Rotenberg, K. J. (Ed.), *Disclosure processes in children and adolescents* (pp. 10–56). New York: Cambridge University Press.

Catalano, R. F., Berglund, M. L., Ryan, J. A., Lonczak, H. S. & Hawkins, J.D. (1999). *Positive youth development in the United States: Research findings on evaluations of positive youth development programs.* Report to the US Department of Health and Human Services, Office of the Assistant Secretary for Planning and Evaluation and National Institute for Child Health and Human Development. Carnegie Council on Adolescent Development. New York: Carnegie Corporation of New York.

Cauce, F. (1994). Social support during adolescence: Methodological and theoretical considerations. In Nestman & Hurrelmann, K. (Eds.), *Social networks and social support in childhood and adolescence* (pp. 89–110). New York: de Gruyter.

Centers for Disease Control and Prevention (2009). *School Connectedness: Strategies for Increasing Protective Factors among Youth.* Atlanta, GA: US Department of Health and Human Services.

Connors, K. E. (1998). Conflict Resolution & Recognition of Diversity via an Art Experience. *Journal of Art & Design Education,* 17(3), 275–282.

Conrad, D. (2004). Exploring risky youth experiences: Popular theater as a participatory, performative research method. *International Journal of Qualitative Methods,* 3(1), 12–25.

Cooper, M. & Sjostrom, L. (2006). *Making art together: How collaborative art-making can transform kids.* Boston, MA: Beacon Press Books.

Davis, K. (2010). Coming of age online: The developmental underpinnings of girls' blogs. *Journal of Adolescent Research,* 25(1), 145–171.

Durlak, J. A. & Weissberg, R. P. (2007). *The impact of after-school programs that promote personal and social skills.* Chicago, IL: Collaborative for Academic, Social, and Emotional Learning.

Eccles, J. S. & Barber, B. L. (1999). Student council, volunteering, basketball, or marching band: What kind of extracurricular involvement matters? *Journal of Adolescent Research,* 14, 10–43.

Eccles, J. S. & Gootman, J. A. (Eds.). (2002). *Community programs to promote positive youth development.* Committee on Community-Level Programs for Youth. Board on Children, Youth, and Families, Commission on Behavioral and Social Sciences and Education, National Research Council and Institute of Medicine. Washington, DC: National Academy Press.

Elliot, D. & Voss, H. (1974). *Delinquency and dropout.* Lexington, MA: Lexington Books.

Erikson, E. H. (1968). *Identity, youth, and crisis* (1st ed.). New York: W.W. Norton.

Ethier, K. A., Kershaw, T. S., Lewis, J. B., Milan, S., Niccolai, L. M. & Ickovics, J. R. (2006). Self-esteem, emotional distress and sexual behavior among adolescent females: Inter-relationships and temporal effects. *Journal of Adolescent Health*, 38(3), 268–274.

Fehr, B. (2004). Intimacy expectations in same-sex friendships: A prototype interaction-pattern model. *Journal of Personality and Social Psychology*, 86, 265–284.

Fredricks, J. A. & Eccles, J. S. (2005). Developmental benefits of extracurricular involvement: Do peer characteristics mediate the link between activities and youth outcomes? *Journal of Youth and Adolescence*, 34(6), 507–520.

Frey, C. U. & Röthlisberger, C. (1999). Social support in healthy adolescents. *Journal of Youth & Adolescents*, 25(1), 17–31.

Gardiner, J. K. (1981). On female identity and writing by women. *Critical Inquiry*, 8(2), 347–361.

Grabe, S., Ward, L. M. & Hyde, J. S. The role of the media in body image concerns among women: A meta-analysis of experimental and correlational studies. *Psychological Bulletin*, 134(3), 460–476.

Grossman, J.B. & Tierney, J.P. (1998). Does mentoring work?: An impact study of the Big Brothers Big Sisters Program. *Evaluation Review*, 22, 403–426.

Guttmacher Institute. (2006). In brief: Facts on American teens' sexual and reproductive health. New York.

Guzzetti, B. J. & Gamboa, M. (2004). Zines for social justice: Adolescent girls writing on their own. *Reading Research Quarterly*, 39(4), 408–436.

Hahn, A., Leavitt, T. & Aaron, P. (1994). *Evaluation of the Quantum Opportunity Program (QOP): Did the program work?* Waltham, MA: Brandeis University, Heller Graduate School.

Hall, G. S. (1904). *Adolescence: Its psychology and its relations to physiology, anthropology, sociology, sex, crime, religion and education.* New York: D. Appleton and Company.

Hetland, L., Winner, E., Veenema, S. & Sheridan, K. (2007). *Studio thinking: The real benefits of visual arts education.* New York:

Teacher's College Press.

Howard, D. E., Wang, M. Q. & Yan, F. (2007). Psychological factors associated with reports of physical dating violence among US adolescent females. *Adolescence, 42*(166), 311–24.

Impett, E. A., Schooler, D. & Tolman, D. L. (2006). To be seen and not heard: Femininity ideology and adolescent girls' sexual health. *Archives of Sexual Behavior, 35*(2), 129–142.

Kaestle, C. E., Halpern, C. T., Miller, W. C. & Ford, C. A. (2005). Young age at first sexual intercourse and sexually transmitted infections in adolescents and young adults. *American Journal of Epidemiology, 161*(8), 774–784.

Larson, R.W. (2000). Toward a psychology of positive youth development. *American Psychologist, 55,* 170–183.

Larson, R.W., Hansen, D. & Walker, K. E. (2005). Everybody's gotta give: Development of initiative and teamwork within a youth program. In Mahoney, J. L., Larson, R. W. & Eccles, J. S. (Eds.). *Organized activities as contexts of development: Extracurricular activities, after-school and community programs.* Mahwah, NJ: Lawrence Erlbaum Associates.

Larson, R. & Richards, M. H. (1994). *Divergent realities: The emotional lives of mothers, fathers, and adolescents.* New York: Basic Books.

Maccoby, E. E. (1988). Gender as a social category. *Developmental Psychology, 24*(6), 755–765.

Maggs, J. L., Patrick, M. E. & Feinstein, L. (2008). Childhood and adolescent predictors of alcohol use and problems in adolescence and adulthood in the National Child Development Study. *Addiction, 103*(s1), 7–22.

Mahoney, J. L. (2000). Participation in school extracurricular activities as a moderator in the development of antisocial patterns. *Child Development,* 71, 502–516.

Mahoney, J. L. & Cairns, R. (1997). Do extracurricular activities protect against early school dropout? *Developmental Psychology,* 33, 241–253.

Mahoney, J. L., Cairns, B. D. & Farmer, T. (2003). Promoting interpersonal competence and educational success through extracurricular activity participation. *Journal of Educational Psychology,* 95, 409–418.

Markus, H. & Nurius, P. (1986). Possible selves. *The American Psychologist,* 41, 954–969.

Marsh, H. W. (1992). Extracurricular activities: Beneficial extension of the traditional curriculum or subversion of academic goals? *Journal of Educational Psychology,* 84, 553–562.

Marti, C. N., Stice, E. & Springer, D. W. (2010). Substance use and abuse trajectories across adolescence: A latent trajectory analysis of a community-recruited sample of girls. *Journal of Adolescence,* 33(3), 449–461.

Maxwell, K. A. (2002). Friends: The role of peer influence across adolescent risk behaviors. *Journal of Youth and Adolescence,* 31(4), 267–277.

McLaughlin, M. W. (2000). Community counts: How youth organizations matter for youth development. Washington, DC: Public Education Network.

McLellan, F. R. (1993). Strengthening adolescent identity formation through development and presentation of family literary documents. Fort Lauderdale, FL: Nova University.

McNelles, L. R. & Connolly, J. A. (1999).

Intimacy between adolescent friends: Age and gender differences in intimate affect and intimate behaviors. *Journal of Research on Adolescence*, 9, 143–159.

Morrison, G. M., Brown, M., D'Incau, B., O'Farrell, S. L. & Furlong, M. J. Understanding resilience in educational trajectories: Implications for protective possibilities. *Psychology in Schools*, 43(1), 19–31.

NCCDPHP. (2005). NCCDPHP, Youth risk behavior surveillance system http://nccd.cdc.gov/YouthOnline/App/QuestionsOrLocations. aspx?CategoryId=C3 (2005).

O'Donnell, L., O'Donnell, C.R. & Stueve, A. (2001). Early sexual initiation and subsequent risks among urban minority youth: The reach for health study. *Family Planning Perspectives*, 33(6), 268–275.

Office of Educational Research and Improvement (OERI). (1993). *Single sex schooling: Perspectives from practice and research*. Washington DC: US Department of Education. In Bertram, C., Hall, J., Fine, M. & Weiss, L. (2000). Where the girls (and women) are. *American Journal of Community Psychology*, 28(5), 731–755.

O'Neill, Shannon Kathleen (2003). Body image among women of color and white women: A meta-analysis. PhD dissertation, State University of New York at Albany. Retrieved March 29, 2011, from Dissertations & Theses: Full Text. (Publication No. AAT 3098302).

Ornstein, A. C. & Levine, D. U. (2008). International education. In *Foundations of Education* (10th ed., pp. 446–470). Boston, MA: Houghton Mifflin.

Oyserman, D., Bybee, D., Terry, K. & Hart-Johnson, T. (2004). Possible selves as roadmaps. *Journal of Research in Personality*, 38, 130–149.

Pajares, F. (2003). Self-efficacy beliefs, motivation and achievement in writing: A review of the literature. *Reading & Writing Quarterly*, 19, 139–158.

Pearson, J., Muller, C. & Wilkinson, L. (2007). Adolescent same-sex attraction and academic outcomes: The role of school attachment and engagement. *Social Problems* 54(4), 523–542.

Peterson, E. A. & Jones, A. M. (2001). Women, journal writing, and the reflexive process. *New Directions for Adult and Continuing Education*, 90, 59–67.

Pfeiffer, J. W. & Jones, J. E. (1975). Introduction to the structured experiences section. In Jones, J. E. & Pfeiffer, J. W. (Eds.), *The 1975 annual handbook for group facilitators* (pp. 3–5). San Diego, CA: Pfeiffer & Company.

Pfieffer, J. W. & Jones, J. E. (1983). *A Handbook of Structured Experiences for Human Relations Training* (Vols. 1–5). La Jolla, California: University Associates.

Philips, D., Linington, L. & Penman, D. (1999). *Creative writing and mental health*. London: Jessica Kingsley Publishers.

Phinney, J. S. (1991). Ethnic identity and self-esteem: A review and integration. *Hispanic Journal of Behavioral Sciences*, 13(2), 193–208.

Piaget, J. (1981). *The psychology of intelligence*. Totowa, NJ: Littlefield, Adams.

Radmacher, K. & Azmitia, M. (2006). Are there gendered pathways to intimacy in early adolescents' and emerging adults' friendships? *Journal of Adolescent Research*, 21, 415–448.

Ragozzino, K., Resnik, H., Utne-O'Brien, M. & Weissberg, R. P. (2003). Promoting academic achievement through social and emotional learning. *Educational Horizons,* 81(4), 169–171.

Ravelin, T. Kylmä, J. & Korhonen, T. (2006). Dance in mental health nursing: A hybrid concept analysis. *Issues in Mental Health Nursing,* 27(3), 307–317.

Reis, H. T. & Shaver, P. (1988). Intimacy as an interpersonal process. In S. Duck, D. F. Hay, S. E. Hobfoll, W. Ickes & B. M. Montgomery (Eds.), *Handbook of personal relationships: Theory, research and interventions.* (pp. 367–389). Oxford, England: John Wiley & Sons.

Rhodes, J. & Spencer, R. (2005) Someone to watch over me: Mentoring programs in the after-school lives of children and adolescents. In Mahoney, J. L., Larson, R. W. & Eccles, J. S. (Eds.). *Organized activities as contexts of development: Extracurricular activities, after-school and community programs.* Mahwah, New Jersey: Lawrence Erlbaum Associates.

Rubin, K. H., Bukowski, W. M. & Parker, J. G. (2006). Peer interactions, relationships, and groups. In Eisenberg, N., Damon, W. & Lerner, R. M. (Eds.), *Handbook of child psychology: Social, emotional, and personality development* (6th ed., Vol. 3, pp. 571–645). Hoboken, NJ: John Wiley.

Spencer, S. J., Steele, C. M. & Quinn, D. M. (1999). Stereotype threat and women's math performance. *Journal of Experimental Social Psychology,* 34, 4–28.

Streitmatter, J. (1999). *For girls only: Making a case for single-sex schooling.* Albany, NY: State University of New York Press.

Weisman, S. A. & Gottfredson, D. C. (2001). Attrition from after school programs: Characteristics of youth who drop out. *Prevention Science,* 2, 201–205. In Durlak, J. A. & Weissberg, R. P. (2007). *The impact of after-school programs that promote personal and social skills.* Chicago, IL: Collaborative for Academic, Social, and Emotional Learning.

White House Council on Women and Girls (2011). *Women in America: Indicators of social and economic well-being.* Retrieved 28 April 2011 from: http://www.whitehouse.gov/sites/default/files/rss_viewer/Women_in_America.pdf

Willis, T. A., Resko, J. A., Ainettte, M. G. & Mendoza, D. (2004). Role of parent support and peer support in adolescence use: A test of mediated effects. *Psychology of Addictive Behaviors,* 18(2), 122–134.

Wilson, G. T., Becker, C. B. & Heffernan, K. (2003). Eating disorders. In Mash, E. J. & Barkley, R. A. (Eds.), *Child psychopathology* (2nd ed., pp. 687–715). New York: Guilford.

Youniss, J., McLellan, J. A., Su, Y. & Yates, M. (1999). The role of community service in identity development: Normative, unconventional, and deviant orientations. *Journal of Adolescent Research,* 14, 248–261.

Youniss, J., Yates, M. & Su, Y. (1997). Social integration: Community service and marijuana use in high school seniors. *Journal of Adolescent Research,* 12, 245–262.

Zimmerman, B. J. (2000). Self-efficacy: An essential motive to learn. *Contemporary Educational Psychology,* 25(1), 82–91.

Other program curriculum support available from The Leadership Program at www.tlpnyc.com/leadership-marketplace.

HERstory: Student Writing Companion

Boys 2 MENtors: Curriculum Manual

Boys 2 MENtors: Student Workbook

Empowering Upstanders: A School-Based Bullying Prevention Program

Empowering Upstanders: Student Workbook

Leadership Skills: High School Manual: Violence Prevention Project

Leadership Skills: High School Workbook: Violence Prevention Project

Leadership Skills: Middle School Workbook: Violence Prevention Project

Leadership Skills: Middle School Manual: Violence Prevention Project